T0277532

THE SUMMIT MINDSET

"A beautiful book and testament to business and life. Written from the heart to be authentic and faith filled, which is how I know Scott Miller lives his life. As I read this book, I could visualize him passionately speaking about the Summit Mindset and the North Star, and I thought about how he and I reached the summit together. I know this book can help others get there, too."

—**JERRY REDA,** president and COO, Big Geyser, Inc.

"A practical and powerful guide to living that's both personally and professionally transformative. Scott's experience, unique insights, and ability to simplify and outline a 360 approach in ascending the summit is exceptional. A must-read for all, from students to C-level executives."

—**CHUCK CZERKAWSKI,** former CFO, Essentia Water

"What if you could quickly learn business and life lessons from someone who has already successfully traveled those roads? *The Summit Mindset* offers common sense direction, seasoned with real-life examples that Scott Miller has gathered over his amazing career. Miller and his writing partner James Moore provide a roadmap for individuals or companies wanting to get to the summit. And stay there."

—**CARY PFEFFER,** author, *There's Not an App for That*

"*The Summit Mindset* is a must-read for any professional who wants to achieve the loftiest of goals building their career. Scott Miller not only has the Summit Mindset, but he also lives it, and resides at the summit. This is a life-changing book with literal recipes that will bring you to the summit."

—**MARK BALOK,** former senior vice president, Glaceau Vitamin Water

"Scott's done an amazing job capturing the insights he's gathered over his highly successful career. His Summit Philosophy on leading a successful organization is thoughtful, practical, and can be applied to anyone's business or personal life. I really enjoyed finding nuggets of wisdom in every chapter."

—**MIKE WEINSTEIN,** former CEO, Snapple Beverage Group

"At a fundamental level, the Summit Mindset way of living is about happiness. And that gives this book a powerful purpose. Scott's insights into eight important habits provides such valuable reminders, and the context around these habits and how they facilitate happiness is brilliant. In the closing chapter, he also distills down the importance of purpose, relationships, self-care, and the courage to ask ourselves hard questions leading to self-reflection. I will return to this book again and again."

—**ZOLA KANE,** chief marketing officer, Essentia Water

THE
SUMMIT
MINDSET

THE
SUMMIT
MINDSET

WINNING THE BATTLE OF YOU VERSUS YOU

SCOTT MILLER & **JAMES C. MOORE**

GREENLEAF
BOOK GROUP PRESS

Published by Greenleaf Book Group Press
Austin, Texas
www.gbgpress.com

Distributed by Greenleaf Book Group

For ordering information or special discounts for bulk purchases, please contact Greenleaf Book Group at PO Box 91869, Austin, TX 78709, 512.891.6100.

Design and composition by Greenleaf Book Group and Mimi Bark
Cover design by Greenleaf Book Group and Mimi Bark
Author photography by Michael Devaney, Sarasota Photographer

Publisher's Cataloging-in-Publication data is available.

Print ISBN: 979-8-88645-074-3

eBook ISBN: 979-8-88645-075-0

To offset the number of trees consumed in the printing of our books, Greenleaf donates a portion of the proceeds from each printing to the Arbor Day Foundation. Greenleaf Book Group has replaced over 50,000 trees since 2007.

Printed in the United States of America on acid-free paper

23 24 25 26 27 28 29 30   10 9 8 7 6 5 4 3 2 1

First Edition

To my family
My wife, Amparo, and my children,
Saige, Storm, and Sloan

Can you remember who you were,
before the world told you who you should be?

—CHARLES BUKOWSKI

CONTENTS

ACKNOWLEDGMENTS

Books, I realized through the process of writing this one, are accumulations and collaborations. They happen because of people in your life and years of experience. Nobody creates a book completely alone. And I am indebted to many people for helping me produce *The Summit Mindset*.

My wife, Amparo, changed my life when she found the courage to move across the ocean and bet on our love. Everything has been positive since we met, and she continually convinces me the best is yet to come. I know I'll always be at the Summit with her by my side, and her support of this project made it possible to realize my vision.

Saige, Storm, and Sloan, my children, I am honored to be your father and proud of all you have taught me. I am sure we will keep creating memories and reminding ourselves of the importance of family, and that it is never about one of us but is always about all of us.

I also owe thanks to my co-author, James Moore, who agreed to collaborate on a type of book he had never written. I discovered, working with him, not just an amazing writer but also an authentic human. I feel honored to have made not just a friend for life, but someone I consider a brother.

Tim Miller has been at my side through all the peaks and valleys leading to the Summit. His brotherhood and friendship have kept me strong with the knowledge I was never alone.

Stacey Miller has also provided the conversations and friendship to create memories with our families and the confidence that comes from caring about each other, and knowing someone is always there when needed.

My cousin Chris Micca provided help reviewing this manuscript, and, although we've been separated by distance for too many years, it has always felt like he was right next door. He has continually been there for me.

I am also honored and grateful to call my cousin Kelly Pascrell, family and friend. Our great conversations have kept my mind stimulated and helped develop this book.

My Irish cousin Tricia Carollo has been supporting all my efforts over the past thirty years. He has continued to remind me that I am never alone. We climbed together toward the Summit, always at each other's side.

I have also been interlocked as a friend and colleague for thirty years with Mark Kent, who has been beside me in business and life. The authenticity and balance he brings to his world have taught me much about becoming a better man. The same is true of Mark Balok, whose wisdom about anything and everything has helped guide me and contribute to what I shared in this book. Both men have been unshakable friends and colleagues through adversity and the good times.

The same is true of Rick Foy. We've often found ourselves snowed in at the Summit, but we've always managed to help dig each other out and keep climbing. We've never left those heights, and his insight has helped to make this a better book.

Bill Scarnaty, a friend of three decades, became a brother over the years, and he has provided excellent feedback on this manuscript as it was being drafted. His thinking improved the manuscript and has always helped me to become a better human.

Valuable and honest feedback also came from my close friend Tom Potenza. Tom has inspired me to improve as a person and businessman. His resiliency and strength through difficult times has always been contagious.

Everyone needs an experienced and talented a mentor to help with their first steps in business and mine was Mike Weinstein. I was only thirty-something when we met, and Mike helped me channel my raw energy into valuable work. He never stopped challenging me and offering critical thinking to help me improve as a person and businessman.

Ken Uptain, a business partner and friend, trusted me with his company, Essentia. I was honored to work alongside such an accomplished individual and help him get his company across the finish line. His patience and persistence taught me much as an entrepreneur. I will always remember the time at Essentia, and it will always inform my business endeavors and my daily life.

The Summit Mindset would have been incomplete without the input of my friend Jerry Reda. We have enjoyed great business conversations and partnerships, which taught us both about the importance of balancing work and family.

Chuck Czerkawski was central to my success at Essentia, and his contributions to this book were also important in forming its messages. He did all the late nights and early mornings, stayed in the fight to the finish line, and is a great friend.

The passionate leadership of Zola Kane, who is great with people and organizations, facilitated much of our success at Essentia and refined my thinking on many subjects in this book. Her authenticity as a leader and a friend made me better each day as an executive and thinker. She was critical at helping shape this book and the culture of success at Essentia.

Kazumi Mechling, "the connector," gave me a clear understanding of the importance of communications in any business and helped define the Essentia workplace culture to be motivational and sustaining. Her introduction to co-author James Moore was an important first step in giving life to this book.

Reid Vokey's contributions to Essentia and this book made them both projects I was proud to be involved with. He taught me about the importance of influencer marketing in the new economy and has used his own influential voice to improve marketing teams' accomplishments all over the world.

I want to also express my love and appreciation for Mel Miller, my daughter-in-law, whose love, laughter, and intelligence made our family stronger and more joyous. My son-in-law, Drew Maltz, offered great critiques and suggestions along the journey of the Summit Mindset and inspired me each day with his persistence and discipline. Kelly Theriault, who had an ability to bring us all closer together as a family, showed us a great approach to life by leading from the front on all our adventures.

Finally, a significant portion of *The Summit Mindset* was drafted and edited in the high desert of West Texas on the Marathon Plateau. Thanks are owed to Daniel Self, who graciously donated the beauty and quietude of his "Rock House" in the Trans-Pecos community of Marathon for the authors' completion of this manuscript.

Scott Miller

INTRODUCTION

Anyone who writes a book needs to explain their motivation by answering a few key questions. And that's where I want to start. Some of the questions are obvious, I guess. Do you have a story to share? Are you going to teach the reader something of value? Why should I buy your book, or even spend time reading it? Is there a purpose for what you are writing? Those are just a few, but I'm not sure that completely gets to why I've decided to jump into this process because creating a book is difficult, and trying to make it valuable to an audience is a complex task. The risk of failure in writing a book, especially one that is intended to help people, is high. There is also the presumption by the writer. Most writers presume they have valuable information and counseling to offer. Who is this guy and why does he think I should listen to him? What good is advice if it goes ignored? But I think it's worth the effort because I believe I can help some people improve their lives and their careers. That can be interpreted as vain, and it's a statement made by many authors, but hang with me here for just a bit and let me offer my quick perspective.

We all learn lessons from others. Might be a mentor or a professor or a counselor or maybe even an investor. Our educations and experiences vary. If we had to acquire all knowledge through daily living and formal education, I think our paths to happiness and success might be delayed. In fact, I'm convinced they would be. Our entire lives might be spent trying to find a fulfillment that evades us because we didn't know how to catch our dreams. My suspicion is, that's why there are so many life coaches and inspirational speakers and self-help books in circulation. Most of us understand that we don't know everything about life and business that could help us achieve our goals. But why stand in the rain and get wet when someone is offering you an umbrella and can provide information on how being chilly and soaked might lead to catching a cold?

What I'm offering in this book takes several forms. Part of it is a prescription for a process and steps you can take to improve personal and professional achievements. Another part involves me sharing stories of my experiences and providing examples and anecdotes of companies and individuals who have fulfilled great ambitions—and a few who have not, so that we might get insights from their failures. These people started, like everyone else, with a dream, and then they discovered practices and developed habits that prepared them to have a shot at success. You may be struggling to find what will work to move you in the direction of your dreams, searching for answers and advice.

And that's why I've written this book.

Much of what is recommended is overcomplicated and not practicable for the life of the average person. My ideas are more viable and practical. You will find simple advice, based on experience and learning, which can help you set a new course or refine your current goals, and find happiness in your daily life.

My education in business came from the ground up, and the principles I learned also worked for my personal life. The first job I got was on the floor of a Pepsi warehouse in New Jersey, which taught me about operations and merchandising. I had acquired a work ethic that came from my family and my parents' struggle to pay the bills, which also gave me the instincts to envision a different life. I didn't want the constant worrying over financial security and end-of-the-month payments I might not be able to make. I was young when I realized that was important, and it prompted me to begin studying performance and process. In my teens and as a young warehouse worker in my twenties, I read constantly to learn about leadership, experimented with better approaches to old functionalities, tried to make tired, old practices more efficient, and, eventually, developed my own methodologies for success.

And they worked.

As the years passed and my career improved, I began to think of my personal process for achievement as a concept I called a Summit Mindset. These were techniques—maybe tactics is a better word—for achievement, paired with my vision, the ideas I had of what I wanted out of life and business, how to get that status and stature, and keep it. I started by always seeing myself on a summit, and I made a conscious decision that nothing was going to knock me down. This "mindset" is an extension of my personal philosophy about achievement and is comprised of standards and practices I always apply to companies and personal development. Regardless of the circumstances I encounter in my life and my job, I can remain on the summit against difficult odds by practicing the techniques and protocols that are consistently effective at improving outcomes for me. I am convinced they will work for anyone, and that's why I wanted to share them in this book.

When you look closely, you can see that success leaves clues. I have constantly analyzed successful businesses and people, even institutions, to see what works, using what I have learned to build an architecture for others. The practices that are included here also come from my experience as an executive and CEO at global beverage companies. Summit Mindset is my program to guide careers, increase the output of companies and grow revenues, make organizations more influential, and improve lives by making happier and more productive people. Any person, institution, or business can increase performance by using the processes and perspective I outline in these pages.

Elements of the Summit Mindset have been tested and refined through years of working in varying business, organizational, and personal environments. Anyone can overcome difficult odds by learning and practicing the techniques I have developed, which have given me great professional and personal success.

The Summit Mindset isn't a magical formulation that quickly turns you into a happy and prosperous person. In this book, I present a series of practical steps that require self-discipline to execute. These steps are not challenging, but they do demand rigorous attention to detail and a focused effort that, for many, will become a way of life. The Summit Mindset has worked, not only in my life and career, but also for colleagues and friends who had struggled to find happiness in their work and personal lives. There has never been anything in my life more important than the pursuit of happiness, and the Summit Mindset has delivered that to me.

And I am confident it can do the same thing for you.

Scott Miller

CHAPTER ONE

YOU VERSUS YOU

Those who say it cannot be done should not interrupt those doing it.

—CHINESE PROVERB

When we begin to focus on personal success, there is a tendency to look for examples, usually people who have achieved in categories relevant to our dreams. You might consider a small business-person who opened a shop and sold a product that became so popular the store had to open several outlets, or was purchased for franchise. Athletes also get a lot of scrutiny for their accomplishments. Yes, they have physical gifts, but such greatness is not merely a product of genetics. Winning invariably is the result of hard work, self-discipline, and an unrelenting vision of a goal, which are all combined with the physical talents provided by nature.

One of the best stories of achievement I've ever encountered comes from the high plains in Kansas. A teenaged farm boy outran all his classmates during gym, so he began to understand before he was twelve years old that he was fast. Coaches at his school noticed too and invited him to join the track and cross-country teams. Even when he ran great distances, his stride was so fast and powerful that his competitors said his heels never touched the ground. The schoolboy quickly became a star, and his coach set him on a training program that was designed to take him beyond the boundaries of his hometown of Wichita and put him on the world stage. The young man embraced that imagery and made it his dream. He dedicated himself to the hard work needed to achieve his vision.

His name was Jim Ryun, and even as a teenager, he was an iconic example of achievement. Ryun's coach convinced him that if he did the necessary training, he had the potential to become the first high schooler in America to break four minutes in the mile. The idea might have been preposterous to a less-determined young athlete, but Ryun dedicated himself to that idea. In 1964, a decade after Dr. Roger Bannister was the first to run an under-four-minute mile, the Kansas kid became the first high school student to accomplish the feat by running the mile in 3:59.

But how, exactly, did he get there?

His base training was to accumulate mileage and build endurance before sharpening his speed with intervals run at race pace or faster. This meant that every morning during those cold Kansas winters, Ryun crawled out of his warm bed and put on gloves, long underwear, sweatpants, shirts, and windbreakers to protect him from the wind, cold, and snow. He ran ten miles each weekday morning before classes with such dependable regularity that local farmers began joking that they set their clocks by his appearance down their roads. After the run, before he caught the school bus, Ryun completed his newspaper delivery route.

Jim Ryun overcame a conflict others might not—the temptation to stay warm and in bed. If we allow it, who we want to be and what we want to achieve can seem like an unconquerable enemy instead of a dream to be fulfilled. People often suggest to us that we adopt more reasonable ambitions and, unsurprisingly, we begin to make compromises, which turn into obstructions standing in the road we want to travel to reach our dreams. Ryun knew he had to confront the weather on those winter mornings and that if he didn't get in his mileage, one of his competitors surely would. He did not decide whether to run each morning by getting out of bed and looking at the weather. Ryun had already made the commitment to put in miles every day before school, regardless of the conditions, because they were essential to his sub-four-minute goal.

What Ryun confronted and overcame is a fundamental internal personal conflict I call "You versus You." But whatever name it might be given, this is not an artificial construct. Whether you are a mid-level manager at your company and hoping to be vice president or a corporate CEO, or you are a teenaged lead singer in a garage band who has notions of recording contracts and massive concert crowds, you must overcome yourself, and, yes, maybe you are a skinny-legged Kansas schoolboy who thinks he can win a medal at the Olympics. Our perceived limitations are tough opponents.

But they can be defeated.

The greatest obstacles to any achievement may lie in the conflicts within us. We must overcome reliance on external influences and opinions. We must break free from the constraints we have placed on ourselves because of teaching or experience. The "You" that you are has to find the right approach to become the "You" that you want to be. This challenge requires you to recognize what's holding you back. A child who wants to become an astronaut as an adult, for example, might live in a home with parents who are unfamiliar with scholarships, grants, or work-study programs. If the parents have not been exposed to a culture that offers such opportunity, the odds are reduced that their children will get the educational opportunities available to them.

As any child comes of age, they must overcome learned responses they picked up from their parents and the guardrails the parents subconsciously placed around the route to their offspring's future. These constraints tend to have no basis in the child's individual makeup or potential to rise into the stars, but culture and economics are often allowed to become destiny.

They don't have to be, though. Jim Ryun never let anything stop him from fulfilling his bold vision of running success, even though he grew up with a farm boy's existence of obscurity on the Kansas plains. He ran in three Olympics, won a medal, and earned world records that stood for years. His career concluded with election to the US Congress and service to his community.

You versus You is at the heart of what each of us will become. As teens, many of us have an idea of what we want to become but sabotage our chances by focusing on the weaknesses and challenges that might prevent us from fulfilling these dreams. This internal battle requires a determination and practical steps to overcome the tendencies to doubt ourselves or to blame the world for getting in our way. We rationalize changes in our goals and accept more practical dreams, instead of focusing on developing the skills and characteristics that will lead to success. We surrender, too soon and unnecessarily, to the lesser outcome.

The Summit Mindset grew out of the understanding I acquired through experience and study of what holds us back. That experience has shown me that people are too quick to accept limiting definitions of themselves and give up too easily before they even discover what they can do. When we force ourselves to confront limitations we have accepted as fact, we can then identify the barriers between where we are now and where we'd love to be. Most of our goals are achievable if we are willing to do the necessary work. Don't misunderstand me. There is more to this than simply speaking our dreams into reality. We *work* them into existence, not think them into being.

As a fundamental requirement of success, it is important to identify our personal strengths and weaknesses and then lay out a path that is paved with strategic thinking, hard effort, and a detailed vision.

One of the most important revelations I had was that many people do not have a purpose, and without one you are adrift. Have you ever met someone who is gifted with great intellect and personality and, somehow, they are a mess? I always wondered how that happens. These types can end up aimless, and I realized that's where dysfunction starts. The Summit Mindset will show you how to avoid that fate with processes that help you make deposits into the equity account of who you are and want to become. We do not have assets that are more valuable than ourselves, and when we do the work to add to that value, it makes us feel alive.

I think constantly about the value of work, but especially in the fall when the leaves begin to turn colors. Autumn was a time of year that created great anxiety for my family. My father was a roofer, and when the snow began to fly, there was no more work, which meant we had no money. He had to scramble to find day jobs to provide for his wife and children until the seasons changed again and he was able to return to regular employment on the rooftops of the Northeast. Many of his days were spent without paid employment, but he was always checking with businesses and looking for a full-time job. Dad started work very young, at the age of twelve after his father left the family. Seven children had to be fed and housed, and a big part of that responsibility was on his shoulders.

I was the same age when a similar burden was passed to me, though not because my father had left his family. No man ever worked harder or took his responsibility of caring for his wife and children more seriously than my dad. He always asked for extra hours and overtime and came home bent and almost too tired to eat after some of his workdays. Not even a completed high school education had been possible for him after his father departed. I was enlisted as a worker for our household by my mother, who struggled to pay the heating bills and buy groceries with what Dad was able to earn. Because I was the oldest child, I was close to the economic anxiety of my parents and took jobs shoveling snow and delivering newspapers and anything that might turn up in our town.

Mom often couldn't afford to pay for the oil for home heating, though, and we spent many school mornings standing by the stove trying to warm up. I was frustrated and angry while not yet a teenager. My family was poor, and it made me feel inferior, which we were not. Our efforts and hard work did not change our living conditions. We lived across the street from the Passaic River, and when spring floods came, the water rose into our house. My father was proud, though, and refused fire department orders to leave. I remember when the water receded, we were left with the task of cleaning away the stench and chasing out rats as big as cats.

Few of us are born to privilege, and work is essential to our daily lives. To know my background, though, is to understand my motivation for developing the Summit Mindset and offering ideas of hope and accomplishment, regardless of our individual origin stories. I think my family's economic struggle made me feel as though I were inadequate, even though we were all doing hard and honorable work, especially my father. Our American culture too often ignores the potential of economically marginalized people and their families, and I felt that pain daily when I was young. Frequently, my father was angered by his inability to make financial progress, and he smoked—he said to calm his nerves—up to three packs of unfiltered cigarettes a day. The habit dramatically shortened his time with his family and led to a moment that informed all that followed in my life.

Cancer, inevitably, got my dad. When he was unable to keep down his food and was without energy, my mom and I took him to the doctor. A biopsy showed an inoperable tumor in his throat that was the size of a lemon and extended into the wall of his stomach. Dad elected to not undergo chemo and asked to go home with his family. That day was my birthday, and when my father awoke from sedation, he wished me a happy birthday even though I was certain he sensed what he was facing. We took him home, and my brother, sister, mother, and I cared for him with an expression of love we tried to make equal to what he had shown us with his hard work and unfailing commitment to his family. My fifty-year-old father, lean and muscular, always proud and independent, lay helpless as he shriveled to sixty pounds in his final hours.

I sat alone with him his last morning, and he felt a need to apologize. I didn't understand what he was feeling.

"I'm sorry," he said.

"For what, Dad?"

"I should've tried harder."

I had no context for his apology. No man had ever tried harder. In fact, I think the greatest lesson I learned from my father's example was that there is nothing more important than trying. We all fail. Failing is learning how to succeed. But we must keep trying. Effort is what defines us. My father's character, his willingness to do whatever was necessary to care for those he loved, is the most instructive lesson I have ever received. Whatever dreams he had cultivated as a young man had to be laid aside to provide for his family, and he did not hesitate to offer us his earnings. He defined fatherhood for me, and love.

A few hours after his apology, Dad asked me to go get Mom from the kitchen. My siblings and I were with our parents when Dad's great heart stopped. We all cried, but not only for our loss. My tears were prompted by his constant struggle and his abiding embarrassment and frustration that he could not offer a better life to his family. I am sure he despised our poverty and his sense of inferiority to those with greater economic means. I hated that he had to know that hurt, and I made a decision as I sat against a wall outside and wept. I was only in my early twenties, but I resolved that my father's struggle would be the example that guided my career and every goal I had for a happier existence. I wanted to be able to help not only my family, but also others who labored to pay their bills and feed and house their families. I just didn't know how.

My belief, since that day, is that we all are confronted with challenging circumstances, and they only vary in their degree of difficulty. Those obstacles, though, are what enable us to evolve and grow as humans and, yes, as business operators and dreamers of great things. My experience proves to me, as the writer Ernest Hemingway said, "The world breaks us all. But those of us who mend are stronger in our broken places." When you use the hurt, you can change and improve. Honesty about ourselves—who we are, what we want, what our failings are—lead us to advance toward our dreams.

I know because it is what my father's life taught me.

Learning to use the hurt is an important part of what the Summit Mindset is about, too. Those difficult experiences with my family formed the principles that have guided me. My contention is that we are responsible for ourselves and what we believe. This is such a strong conviction with me that I don't even consider the idea that there are victims in business or professional achievement. I think there are only volunteers. I certainly don't mean to suggest that people choose to fail or there is no such thing as victimization. But if we do not try or put in the required effort, planning, and detail work for personal improvement and advancement, we make failure almost inevitable. How to avoid such an outcome and accomplish important life goals is what you will learn from the processes of the Summit Mindset.

Before I go any further, though, it's important to offer an overview of the Summit Mindset. While some of the basic concepts are obvious, the strength of my approach to a happy life and a successful career relies on consistency, a productive form of repetition. I constantly tell people that to achieve their dreams, they must "do the reps." I suppose, through the years, that has become a mantra associated with me by people with whom I've worked and, yes, even my friends. The truth is, though, nothing is achievable without consistent performance, over and over and over. This repeated behavior will prepare you for success and the survival of hardship. Habits build confidence, and consistent small steps can create a long and fulfilling journey.

My approach acknowledges that none of us escape the rain. Struggles are inevitable, even for the most blessed of people, which is why we all need purpose. Usually, this is a recognition or acknowledgment of what brings us happiness. Then we begin our pursuit. We will almost certainly fail at times along the way, but struggle is our teacher. Even when we accomplish our goals, it is important to remain constructively analytical, constantly reviewing the tape, finding what we might do better, and learning how to grow and evolve. The need to constantly recalibrate in life is critical. We should be physically and mentally prepared for climate changes, whether we are already at our summit or busily climbing.

The Summit Mindset is not a philosophy. I see it as almost an owner's manual to help people live a happy, fulfilled life, or to assist leaders in businesses and communities achieve meaningful changes. I think it facilitates the genesis of a positive spirit and teaches us to live in gratitude. Consider the sheer miracle of being alive, the astronomical odds that came together to create you. When we acknowledge that most basic of gifts, we are more compelled to take advantage of what we can offer the world, and we will discover, in return, what it wants to offer us. That thinking is the pulse that beats in the Summit Mindset.

Exercises:

- **You versus You:** Create your dream scenario. What would happen for you if you had complete control over your life's outcomes? Now make a list of personal attributes that would make this fantasy arrive. Are you smart? A hard worker? Is focus a problem? Make two columns with a list of positive and negative characteristics about yourself and consider which ones would help you arrive at your dream goal. Pick out the hurtful ones on your list, which have the potential to disrupt your plans. Can you do something to eliminate each of these to improve your chances for success? Or do you need to work around them? Examine a previous failure in your life. Was there something you might have done differently to change that outcome? Parse your list of positive attributes by selecting those that will be most valuable in the pursuit of your dream job or place of greatest happiness. Are there other skills you can develop to facilitate the realization of your dreams? Is more education required? Write a few paragraphs analyzing one of your life's biggest successes and detail what contributed to the achievement. Use the same exercise with a failure and try to determine what happened and why.

- **The Inside-Out:** Ask the most fundamental question possible: *Who am I?* Do you know? What ideas do you have about what type of person you want to become? Or are you happy as you are? If so, what provides that happiness? Does a religious faith guide your daily life? Are you spiritual and giving? Do you think about other people or are you generally focused on the health and well-being of you and your family? What do you do with your free time? Are your primary interests financial or social? Are sports important? Do you think we are all obligated to help one another? How important is fulfilling work to you? Have you been able to maintain a work-life balance? Do you make personal sacrifices for your career? Is family the most important element of your life? How important are your friends? Have you known since you were young what you wanted to do with your life? Do you feel guilt easily? These are just a few questions worth asking as you search for an understanding of self, which when completed, will help set you on a course guided by your character and principles.

CHAPTER TWO

FINDING YOUR NORTH STAR

It's about finding your values and committing to them. It's about finding your North Star. It's about making choices. Some are easy. Some are hard. And some will make you question everything.

—TIM COOK, APPLE

Serendipity is not a plan for success. Trips are meaningless without a destination, aren't they? We don't get in the car and just drive around and then return home. The purpose of travel is to arrive at a location we have chosen for various reasons. It's an incisive metaphor for life, too. If we don't have goals and ideas on how they are achieved, aren't we just wandering while doing our daily activities? How can you make progress toward a destination you have not yet identified? Even without clearly defined ambitions, we need to determine our principles and purposes as an individual, which will simplify the job of establishing our dreams.

Our lives need a North Star, a purpose that guides us on a fulfilling course. Your North Star is brightened by a clarity of purpose that includes intentions and actions that lead to a predetermined achievement. We hang the star in our personal sky by answering questions about what we want to be and where we'd like to go. We can't achieve excellence without this type of guidance. If, for instance, you want to become a published writer, you need to write and keep improving until your writing is strong enough to be shared. Ask any commercially published author about how they reached that level of writing and the one word that is likely to be spoken is *perseverance*. A wise writer, published or not, is perpetually trying to become better, even after being named a Nobel Laureate. There is no finish line for a writer, and that's true for whatever North Star any of us chooses.

The idea that there is no finish line might be difficult to accept, but it has been a sustaining and inspirational concept for me. We need to keep going toward new horizons and goals, and the accomplishment of a short-term task or milepost ought to spur us onward to even greater achievements. If there were a finish line, what might come next? Do we find a place on the beach and stare at the ocean? That is certainly rewarding for almost any length of time, but can it fire our souls? Where does our motivation for life and achievement then originate? Don't we all need projects and dreams that get us out of the bed in the morning and give us a purpose?

Think also about what the North Star analogy can mean to an organization or an enterprise. The North Star offers guidance for everyone who is a part of that institution. The concept aligns closely with a company's brand image; how does the consumer or the broader marketplace perceive what you offer? If your staff is working together to reach a common North Star, the outside world will take note. Mercedes-Benz has a long-held goal of being the world's leading luxury vehicle, dependable and safe with desirable accessories and a sales and service network that responds to customers who can afford the automotive manufacturer's exceptionalism. Product advertising and sales collaterals reflect this carefully calculated image, which is the Mercedes North Star. BMW and Cadillac are involved in similar ambitions, as are various other vehicle producers. Think of all the brand names that are familiar and the image their products immediately conjure. These are companies that know what they are about and are consistently led toward their North Star. The result? Financial success.

Is it risky for a company to ignore this concept? Well, there certainly are examples of bad things happening when they do, and one case is historic in American business lore. Some of you reading this may have never even heard of the Eastman Kodak Company, which later became Kodak Film. They were a dominant American business for a century and by 1968 had captured 80 percent of the global market share of photography before they made one of the biggest blunders in business history. Instead of adapting to create technologies that used digital photography, Kodak believed consumers would never abandon film cameras. The leadership team consistently argued against changing the film-based revenue model, even after Kodak engineer Steve Sasson invented the first digital camera in 1975 and brought his creation to the attention of the executive suite. The very technology that was to kill an American legacy enterprise was born within its walls and was ignored.

"But it was filmless photography," inventor Sasson explained to a reporter. "So, management's reaction was, 'That's cute, but don't tell anyone about it. That's how you shoot yourself in the foot.'"

Ignoring disruptive technology, invented by your own company, is not a wise strategy for winning in the marketplace. Kodak had achieved historically massive revenues by implementing what is often referred to as the *razor and blades* business plan. The razor is sold for a low profit margin, but consumables like razor blades make considerably more money because of recurrent purchases and low costs of production. Kodak sold cameras at relatively affordable prices but made great profits on film, printing sheets, and various other accessories needed to produce quality images. With consistent growth, Kodak executives were able to rationalize decisions to resist the digital movement for decades, but the industry moved past its historic business leader and product developer.

The digital *disease* that killed off Kodak was being manufactured almost before the eyes of the executive team. A key milestone in the advancement of digital photography was the development of the mega-pixel camera, which also came from the research labs of Kodak. The future that was to destroy Kodak—a camera that built images out of millions of tiny dots—was developed by Kodak's own laboratories. Dramatically increasing the number of pixels in an image profoundly improved its color and quality. The company's strategic decision, in the face of advancing tech, however, was to use digital only to improve the quality of film. Kodak denied logic and ignored a study performed by Vince Barraba, head of the company's marketing intelligence division, whose research forecast that the megapixel camera would bring on the advent of standalone digital photography. This transcends irony to become rank stupidity. How does any company so consistently ignore its own research and development? As a manager, I find it hard to imagine how such a thing could have happened.

Contemplate what might have been different had Kodak established a North Star, and it wasn't only about film photography. What if they had thought through their entire business and revenue model, reenvisioned their future, and simply determined they wanted to be the company that made it possible for people to enjoy pictures in whatever format and with whatever technology was most desirable and convenient in the marketplace? How could they have arrived at any other conclusion than the fact that digital pictures were the future of photography? They ought to have determined they were going to provide quality and affordable photography to their customers and do it by the means required to make the experience fun and repeatable. The fact that the executives of Kodak were able to ignore digital advancements by their in-house engineers remains astounding to me. The result of this unwillingness to adapt is that the company filed for Chapter 11 bankruptcy protection in 2012.

There are a thousand ways to write the epitaph of Kodak, I suppose. *"A company creates powerful new technology, but ignores it,"* or *"Giant photo business dies after suppressing potential new markets."* The story is an object lesson in a failure to rely on the basic behaviors I practice with the Summit Mindset. How did management willfully not listen to its own experts on marketing and research and development? If the company had a North Star to be the business I described—provide quality film and devices for photography—why did leadership not see that Kodak needed to be constructively dissatisfied with its status quo? Was there no introspection? Did they never contemplate what they might be doing wrong?

I hate to say this, but common sense is relatively uncommon in business. With a Summit Mindset, the crisis that destroyed Kodak would have been avoided. I advise companies and individuals to begin that work with what I have labeled the *Inside-Out* job. This is inward, honest reflection on who you are and what you want, which leads to a clarity of purpose. Included are questions about, what matters most to you as a person or a business, what do you believe, is there a foundation that you are building upon, and what do you want to become? Asking these things of yourselves might be hard, and answers will include difficult truths for almost everyone, but by consistently exploring them, you can arrive at some revealing conclusions, both comforting and unsettling. But before you can head for your North Star, you need to figure out what defines you. The most effective people know what they want out of life and remain constantly committed to guiding principles, which ultimately create their happiness.

If you aren't there yet, then begin your Inside-Out work.

The value of this self-analysis is to identify your four *pillars*—the four dominant principles you will need to guide your life and remain focused on goals. They set a foundation for the construction of happiness, and in my experience, I have found they are essential for progress and fulfillment, and to keep you pointed in the direction of that North Star. Individuals need pillars as badly as businesses do. When I have interviewed people for leadership roles, I always ask them to define themselves for me, and, amazingly, most people can't answer that basic question. Who are you? What do you want to achieve? When I know these things, I can ask the right questions and learn about a person based upon who they consider themselves to be. I want the people I work with to be inspired to be better humans and employees who are purpose driven. If your four pillars are described to me as *family, business, faith,* and *fitness*, I know you, and I can determine whether you fit with my team. Pillars are not always of the same strength or weight, either. Almost every day one of them increases or decreases, but if you have all four, there is a foundation for returning to the best version of yourself and an unfaltering focus on goals, to perpetually become a better you.

I know this sounds like obvious and logical thinking, but the amazing fact is, most people and businesses never take the time to engage in these important, fundamental processes. I can see no other way to provide clarity in an enterprise, or even a start-up company, without a transparent understanding of purpose, and that achievement requires brutal honesty inside a business or in personal self-analyses. The Inside-Out process needs to involve uncomfortable questions we have avoided asking. I realized how evasive corporate leaders can be on this matter during a company acquisition where I was helping to construct the deal. Both sides of the negotiating table were asking questions about each other's operations to learn more and gain additional confidence prior to the close and signing of paperwork. After listening to honest responses and a few marketing platitudes, I finally asked the purchasers a tough question: "Okay, well, sounds like you are great. But what do you suck at?"

The room went silent. They turned to each other for answers. No one seemed to know the company's weaknesses, or had even bothered to contemplate what they might be and how they affected revenues. Surely, I thought, there had to be some failing, but they continued to talk about their corporate growth and how that was proof they were executing for their shareholders. That's reasonable thinking, I suppose, but every business, and especially corporations that are multinationals, have flaws. Not knowing what they are doesn't make them less harmful to achieving optimal outcomes.

Maybe this giant corporation was bad at managing crisis communications. Many large businesses fail at this critical function because they conclude the public has no right to know internal workings.

What might happen if the consumer product they manufacture were to become poisoned by an outsider, and people were harmed by it? This very tragedy has occurred in American business in the past and has, in fact, caused both consumer and industry harm. Every future dollar a company hopes to earn can be jeopardized by an inadequate response to such a crisis. My guess is the firm I was speaking with had never contemplated such a scenario and probably didn't even have a crisis communication plan on the shelf.

The same is true with people. We have weaknesses; it's what makes us human. But we can work on our weak spots just as a business can root out its suboptimal operations then engineer improvements in either human or technological performances. When I tell people, "Embrace what you suck at," I get strange looks and then questions about what I am trying to communicate. If you perform your Inside-Out work properly, you are certain to come across a failing or two, or a challenge you have managed not to confront. We aren't the only ones who know what we suck at, either. Good friends and colleagues can tell us how we can be better people or professionals if we ask ourselves the hard questions, and then we can ask those who are closest to us. Imagine what might have happened at Kodak if the leadership team had realized it sucked at envisioning a future for photography, and that future was unfolding in the labs right down the hallway from the executive suites. The company's fate might have been entirely different if it had honestly considered what it was doing poorly. If we don't admit what we don't know or acknowledge what we are doing poorly, how do we improve?

I have known executives who refuse to confront their personal short-comings as leaders and believe their business experience is all they need to continue succeeding. Often, it is difficult for accomplished people to acknowledge personal failings. In the C-suite, leaders sometimes don't learn the names of the people who work for their company, those who are carrying out the strategies to compete and grow revenue. The simple act of knowing a person's name offers them empowerment and impor-tance, and yet too many leaders fail at this basic task. Shake their hand the first time, look them in the eye, and repeat their full name. You will remember. Great politicians have turned this skill almost into an art form. President Lyndon Baines Johnson was legendary for his ability to remember names and acquire votes. Campaigning for the US Senate, he was often able to stop on the town square in rural Texas communities and speak to nearly everyone on a first-name basis and ask about their parents and children by name after having met them only once on a previous campaign stop. We need to let people know they matter, because they do. We get better at communication when we say what others need to hear.

The Inside-Out process enables us to review the tape too, which I consider invaluable for learning. We can discover where we messed up, personally or as a business, and learn from those mistakes. Our American culture teaches us that stinking, or, yes, sucking at something, is a weakness, and as a result, our inclination is to not look back at failure. We even ignore or cover up shortcomings we know we need to deal with. By embracing our weaknesses, we can deconstruct what happened, reflect on our mistakes, share them, and get ideas from others as a kind of education for future prevention. This turns a perceived flaw into a strength. You always stink at something. Your business stinks at something, too. Find out what it is. Confront it and recalibrate. I am consistently looking for little nuggets to give me insights. Being aware of what I suck at allows me to keep learning and growing, and that openness to information of all types will help any person or business.

The Inside-Out work is also what helps us develop our strategic pillars. Asking the elemental questions can take us to a profound place of strength. Who am I? What do I want to do? How can I be meaningful and happy? Can productive work help me find happiness? How can I define my future? What guides my life now? What is easy and natural for me? Is helping others a part of my work destination? These are just some of the questions we might ponder as individuals, and the answers can lead to the creation of the four pillars to guide your life toward its North Star. What happens to a business when a range of similar questions is asked by executives and then shared with employees? I can tell you because I have seen the results. It changes things, inevitably, for the better. Employees feel a part of something larger than themselves and their jobs. They are working toward a greater vision of accomplishment, and there is just no overestimating the value of that feeling in an employment setting. People become empowered to make decisions and do good work because they know what will move them and the company closer to its North Star, which will bring more than just monetary rewards.

The empowerment begins with mutual respect and giving those employees a voice. When they are engaged in helping the company to find its pillars and define its future, they develop mutual respect and understand that communication matters to everyone in the organization. Working hard is important, but we all need to know exactly what we are working at. We do this by finding what I describe as *smart actions*. Don't simply put in the time. Work strategically toward a near-term goal while you are also laboring toward that North Star image of your company and its brand. Do something smart every day that moves you a little closer to your North Star. A pursuit of this nature can align with your personal aspirations of happiness. It doesn't have to be a monumental chore; even just following up a phone call or an email with a person who can help is the kind of smart action that moves you onward. Maybe that is someone you met socially, who expressed an interest in your ambitions or your business and had influence or resources that might be of assistance to you. Never be afraid to communicate and even ask for guidance. If that company's North Star, or the executive you might have met, speaks to your individual principles and beliefs, you've probably found the right company to work for, or the perfect mentor. My certain conviction is that we all need to be chasing happiness, and if we are not, we lose the energy to fulfill tasks that work for us and our employers. Sadly, that is incredibly common. I am shocked at how many people I encounter who are distraught over life and say they gave up on happiness a long time ago.

The Summit Mindset prepares you to avoid that kind of collapse. You expect bad things to happen, but you know you will be prepared because you have done the hard work of learning what makes you happy and finding the North Star of your business or your personal life. I can also give you example after example of how Summit Mindset thinking might have saved a business. Probably people who read this will have never heard of the BlackBerry, even though the developer, Research In Motion (RIM), is responsible for the smart phone you might be holding in your hand. The company lacked the processes to adapt and grow in the right direction and missed opportunities to evolve and continue as the market leader.

The BlackBerry wireless device was once almost ubiquitous in American culture. Its development and acceptance were nearly unprecedented and dawned a revolution in how we communicate. A handheld tool for calls, email, messaging, and other data on the internet, the BlackBerry was so sufficiently prevalent in our daily lives that its nickname, the CrackBerry, was a dark allusion to the addictive nature of the device based on a public perception of overreliance. The BlackBerry is generally regarded as the father of the wireless handheld industry but was overtaken by the more innovative iPhone and, eventually, the Android. During its strongest market penetration, though, BlackBerry owned 43 percent of the mobile phone market share in the United States, and 20 percent worldwide.

And then it disappeared.

What happened to the BlackBerry can easily be described as a failure to adhere to a vision, or not bothering to establish one. The contemporary performance of RIM was so impressive that executives paid no heed to the direction in which the smart phone industry was moving. While it may sound like an oversimplification, BlackBerry lacked a North Star and was unwilling to innovate to maintain market dominance. The only considerations for their product went into the contemplation and engineering of minor iterations of functions. The BlackBerry practically created the popularity of the cell phone industry but was not conscious enough of consumer appetites and the technology of the category it had created to innovate its business.

The decline of the BlackBerry was precipitous, and the causes were obvious. According to *Business Insider*, in the fourth quarter of 2016, 423 million smart phones were sold worldwide; BlackBerry accounted for only 207,900 units, which meant their market share was officially just above 0 percent. The company's demise was telegraphed the day Steve Jobs stood on a stage in front of Apple's shareholders and pointed to pictures of BlackBerrys that were cropped to show only the keyboard.

"Their problem is this lower 40 percent," he said. "We are going to eliminate that with our touchscreen."

Unconvinced, the RIM engineers and execs stuck with the keyboard and its tactile appeal to their user base. Surely, feeling the keyboard made more sense than simply touching letters that appeared on a screen. But did BlackBerry leadership research user habits or desires regarding keyboard functionalities? Many BlackBerry users typed quickly without looking at their keyboards, which is the skill acquired by experienced typists. Such an ability seemed unlikely with a touchscreen that, by design, required attention of the eye and lacked real haptics. But did they have data to back up those assertions? BlackBerry made a major miscalculation and began to bleed its market share. There were hurried innovations to the device that included color screens and, finally, a version without a keyboard, but it was too late to save a company that had lost its way. In early 2022, BlackBerry stopped supporting its operating system on its iconic models, and a device that looked like it was changing the world had finally and formally become obsolete. A gigantic business that had a foundational impact on the advent of the smart phone era had simply disintegrated into economic history.

Executives at BlackBerry were complacent and did not confront themselves about their product because they were convinced they had created a unique handheld tool that would sustain its market dominance with only minor improvements. They were wrong. Was there a North Star guiding the engineering and design, sales, manufacturing, and marketing teams? Or were they taking a constant victory lap, congratulating themselves instead of being in a mode of perpetual challenge to improve?

The Summit Mindset, I am confident, could have helped prevent the demise of the BlackBerry and Research In Motion. Leadership teams would have been working toward a broader goal in their industry, a vision obtained through internal scrutiny and shared values that created the strategic pillars to keep them pointed at their North Star. Instead, externally, there appeared to be almost smug satisfaction at product dominance, until it was too late to save the company. Every business needs to be open to possibility, and maybe even game out a few that might cause problems or additional success. But what happened to BlackBerry, in hindsight, seems almost too predictable. The big, fast train of their success was rolling rapidly downhill, and not a soul on board had ever contemplated that a bridge might be out up ahead or the track needed repair. No autopsy of BlackBerry was necessary. Cause of death was readily apparent. The bridge was out, and nobody ever bothered to check the tracks.

All success involves diligent preparation and anticipation.

Exercise:

- **North Star:** What is your North Star? Maybe you are a coach. Do you want to lead young men and women to championships while also making certain you develop leaders and good students who graduate on time? Your North Star might be the perpetual building of a reputation for your school as a place of fine academics and scholar athletes who win and change their communities for the better. Do you have a business that sells industrial tools? Perhaps you are guided by a desire to have the most durable and affordable power instruments that can be used by weekend carpenters and professional builders to create homes and products that people enjoy, while providing jobs and pride in workmanship for your employees. You know your North Star. You've done the work above to analyze and scrutinize yourself and your company. Choose your words carefully and make a statement of purpose. Then, get to work because you know where you are going.

CHAPTER THREE

LIVING OUR PILLARS

Adversity is an opportunity to show great character.
Bad things are good things in disguise.

—GAL SHAPIRA

Americans are fascinated by success. But I think we fail to get the definition correct, to truly understand what it means to be successful. I have always believed that success is about achieving happiness, which does not have to be associated with money. Fulfilling work is an element of success and taking part in something larger than ourselves, which offers meaning to our work and lives. In our country, though, many consider monetary accomplishment to be a birthright. We expect to arrive at a place of financial security and happiness, but we generally don't understand how to get there. It seems terribly complicated. How do I know what I want to do with my life? Am I getting the right kind of education? Will I be able to make connections with people willing to help me? We also add complexity to our lives because we frequently choose professions that pay us a lot of money but don't offer us personal fulfillment. I know many people who quit their jobs midcareer to find a new line of work they hope would make them happier.

But it's not that complicated.

What I discovered as my career unfolded was that there were some obvious tactics to advancement and success, and these are what I am sharing with the Summit Mindset. There was nothing mysterious about what had an impact on my progress toward goals, and I took note of those factors. These simple choices, which came to comprise my personal perspective and habits, were easy to make and consistently created a substantial difference. I decided to always be early for every meeting, as just one example, and told myself that being on time was being late, and if I was late, I had failed. This choice communicates enthusiasm and interest and does not go unnoticed by participants. When I moved into a management role, colleagues realized my expectations, and we wasted no time with late meetings or absent invitees. Being diligent and prompt affects how others view you as a person and as an employee or team member.

I realize that some people might view this approach to leadership and management as a bit hokey, and even call BS. I've heard the criticism before, but I also know from experience that there are basic steps to be taken to improve any organization, and when people are engaged in a system for improvement, it works. A leader can't simply tell his employees that he wants to make his company number one in the world, whatever their industry, and then set them loose to figure out how to get there. Principles are essential and require guidance on how to function better together as a team. Add to these principles your best methods for solving and avoiding problems, and you will create a workplace culture that speaks to something greater than the individual. When a team sees the leadership owning and living by the principles of the culture, they begin to believe, and improvements start to appear.

The Summit Mindset has worked for me, just as it can for you, and each of my employers experienced growth in their businesses through the implementation of my protocols. Those achievements got noticed within the beverage industry where I worked, and just as the economy and the entire population of the US was reeling from the COVID-19 pandemic, I was contacted by a bottled water company about becoming their top executive to expand their market and improve the profile for a potential acquisition. There were certainly better times to move across country and start a new job. People were working from home in huge numbers, offices were shutting down, and contracts were being delayed or canceled in all kinds of businesses. Many industries in hospitality and travel were grinding to a near shutdown, and the federal government was being pressured to intervene. Cultural issues were also straining the social fiber of our country. But I was intrigued, partially because these circumstances would certainly provide a test of the Summit Mindset and its value to individuals and businesses, and it was the kind of business challenge that I found attractive.

My resumé, which is not unlike numerous managers in the beverage business, includes the brands Pepsi, Snapple, Gatorade, Dr Pepper, Yoo-hoo, and Tampico Beverages, a global manufacturer of juice drinks and freezer pops. Those experiences are what caught the attention of the founder and investors of Essentia, a rising national brand in the bottled water sector. Essentia was growing as a *lifestyle* refreshment and was approaching one hundred employees and increasing retail sales. The drink was the first ionized alkaline bottled water provided in the US, which created the category. The company used a process to remove acidity from its water and increase the pH level, which consumers responded to by claiming the taste was better than other commercial waters and with a belief that it provided them greater satisfaction in terms of hydration. Essentia's growth was not simply about marketing and distribution; it had also been driven by an organic demand for a quality product.

The company was founded by Seattle-area entrepreneur Ken Uptain, an entrepreneur with a reputation for being resilient and persistent. He was also known to care greatly for the people who worked for him, which undoubtedly had much to do with why Ken had been successful in construction, real estate, seafood, and sports apparel. He had retired at forty-four but was curious a few years later when he heard about a process to remove acidic ions from water and raise pH levels to improve taste. He was also pleased to hear about how well the consumer felt after drinking water with lower acidic measurements. Because bottled waters that dominated the market were from springs and glaciers and other natural sources, Uptain considered that the time was not yet correct for his non-sourced water idea.

Ken Uptain's business judgment, I learned, had a record of being insightful. His companies had already produced an economic impact in the Seattle area with jobs and investment capital. Born almost with a hammer in his hand, Uptain began framing houses as a carpenter out of high school and built his first home for sale eight years later, which led to a profitable construction company. Eventually, Uptain became friends with a Norwegian who was in Seattle building a fish processing ship and had the same entrepreneurial drive as himself. Banks in Norway had been seeking opportunities to invest capital in the US, and Uptain and his business partner Kjell Inge Røkke became a conduit for loans that financed all types of real estate from shopping centers to apartment complexes. In fifteen years, they became a publicly traded company called Resource Group International that diversified to include owning the brands Frank Shorter running gear, Brooks shoes, and Helly Hansen apparel. Røkke's background in commercial fishing meant the company also included a seafood division called American Seafoods. Uptain did not need to continue working after these successes, but the concept of the higher pH water was continually intriguing and, after a short hiatus from entrepreneurship, he began developing Essentia and its brand image.

"I had a few early missteps," he told me. "I developed a brand strategy in '98 and started doing well enough pretty quickly to sell the company, but then I bought it back several years later. I didn't like what was being done with the brand. So, I took on some private equity and stepped on the gas a bit in 2012 and we started growing. But remember, I'd already had one business career and I didn't think I had the right motivation or experience in that bottled water business to really grow the operation. We were doing pretty good, but I knew it could be better, and I needed help to get there."

Two buyers had made failed attempts to acquire Essentia, in part because of unacceptable purchase prices. Uptain, though, was convinced more value could be added to his company and was equally certain he was not the leader to accomplish that task, which is when a couple of investors suggested we meet and talk about his company. If Essentia was able to increase productivity and expand sales and distributorships, there was a likelihood Uptain might see an attractive offer for acquisition.

Uptain was relying on my thirty years in business, managing large teams and solving complex company problems, to help his bottled water firm expand even further in a brutally competitive industry that accounted for a little under $20 billion in domestic US sales and a global market of more than $215 billion. Bottled water manufacturers were accustomed to profit margins of 50 to 200 percent based upon the low costs of production and acquisition of a readily available resource. What did I think I was going to be able to accomplish to improve the operations of a business like Essentia that was showing continuous revenue growth in the tens of millions and a brand image that was being communicated, spontaneously, by influencers like the Kardashians and musician Taylor Swift, who drank from an Essentia bottle during onstage performances?

I saw immediately that Essentia was a very good company that had potential for greatness, and I was confident my practices could make incremental improvements toward that unstated goal. There was no question that the company had a fine record of accomplishment in its industry. But when I examined Essentia, I realized that, in many ways, the staff and executives didn't know who they were. This is one of the key elements for success in my Summit Mindset. A company and its employees must have a common understanding of who they are and what the company is about, and that goes beyond product and brand. There was no shared purpose at Essentia at that time that I could see everyone striving for, and all organizations must have that, whether they are Apple or Google, or any other company. Essentia had a good product that people liked, and it was selling but missing elements that, if properly instituted, could help it achieve greatness. I was excited to work with Uptain and his senior leadership team to define who we were as a company and identify our North Star by implementing the Summit Mindset.

While much of the country seemed restive over the pandemic and racial injustices, people were looking for leadership in government and business. There were moments that immediately called for a response by businesses and communities to address important issues. I knew that in my new role as CEO at Essentia, our team needed to take steps to help the greater Seattle area, and I had to find a resource to assist our employees as they and their families dealt with the pandemic. One of the key principles of the Summit Mindset is to create generations of servant leaders—people focused on both business achievement and giving back to their communities. Some of the first meetings I had with the senior leadership team were to discuss and plan that effort. Three days after my arrival, a Minnesota man, George Floyd, an African American, was murdered by a White police officer who kept his knee on Floyd's neck until he suffocated. Our team, led by marketing and corporate communications, was prompted by that tragedy to send a message of inclusion and support to the Seattle area. The consensus of our group was advice to make significant six-figure, impactful donations to African American organizations within our community, which included the United Negro College Fund, the Urban League, and the Black Voters Matter organization.

"I really didn't believe a donation of that size would ever be possible," Chief Marketing Officer Zola Kane said afterward. "The company had never done anything of that significance in terms of community. We put together a program quickly, almost over the weekend, and made a very direct statement that our company was against what had happened, and we were going to make a real effort to be a part of making things better. The leadership team, the company in general, was empowered to do something meaningful. When I was told the amount, my mouth actually fell open, and as word got around the company, there was a great sense of pride and community. I can honestly say it had a huge positive effect on everyone who worked there. We were all so proud."

The George Floyd incident also prompted me to begin my time as the new executive leader, speaking to our staff of a few hundred employees about diversity. We organized small group meetings of five people to discuss diversity of cultures and ethnicities and ideas. My sense has always been that we process information and experiences differently because of our backgrounds, and awareness of those differences will improve cooperation, understanding, and productivity. There was no way that I, as a White male, was ever going to know what a Black or Hispanic person experienced as a victim of racial profiling. But I wanted to understand better and so did our employees, and they had an urgent need to talk about how they felt. People want to be empowered and given a voice, and these meetings began a connection among our employees that offered a kind of healing that was needed because of what was happening beyond their control. I saw the employees became more engaged as leaders.

The Summit Mindset teaches that adversity is inevitable for people and companies. We are all tested and need to be prepared. In a business environment, that means coming together to plan how to overcome obstacles, which is the same demand to be made on a person. We should make ourselves ready for the challenges that are predictable in every life. The prescription for taking those steps varies based upon circumstances, but what was apparent to me after just a matter of days at Essentia was an untapped enthusiasm for contributing, helping others, and becoming more than a drink company. There were other dynamics at work too, which needed to be implemented in making the company greater. I got the unmistakable impression the entire organization was eager to listen and learn and act.

I decided the best way to begin the process of bringing the company together in a unified direction was to call a meeting and establish our strategic pillars. The senior leadership team went to a whiteboard and created several sets of four pillars to serve as the foundation of the company and guide employees in creating a strong culture, moving toward what we chose as our North Star. After multiple revisions, we brought several sets of our pillars to a company meeting and put them on a screen at a town hall–style format. I opened the floor for discussion and, ultimately, sent out the groups of pillars chosen by employees to be voted on for adoption. Cultural habits must be defined, offering standards for work and personal behavior, to avoid becoming a meaningless plaque on a boardroom wall, gathering dust as it goes ignored. My goal was to facilitate an entrepreneurial spirit and a sense of urgency that would turn our organization into an overachieving culture.

Our North Star was obvious to everyone in the room, and we chose the pursuit of being the number one premium water in the global marketplace. By consensus, we selected four strategic pillars:

1. **People First:** Become one team; enable people to have a voice and be their authentic self.

2. **Essentia Nation:** Have the grit of an underdog; exercise inclusivity by welcoming everyone's thoughts, gender identity, and ethnicity.

3. **Overachieving Culture:** Focus on smart action, decisiveness, and accountability, thinking and acting like an entrepreneur, robust communications.

4. **Pursue Goal of Becoming Number One Premium Global Water:** Lead from the front with a revolutionary spirit, relentlessly challenging ourselves in all we do.

We had produced a recipe for a desired culture of achievement. I was pleased with the employee decisions for ambitious goals and was certain they would point us in a positive direction for the company's production and brand, while also creating a work environment that people enjoyed. The senior leadership team had a sense of urgency, and it was quickly communicated to staff, who adopted the same attitude.

Reid Vokey Sr., who was the manager of sponsorship marketing at Essentia, admitted surprise at these fundamental guidelines and habits and the impacts they had within the company.

"I thought what was interesting was that we began to communicate and collaborate at a level that I had not experienced," he explained. "And people were very intent, once that began to happen, on not losing that high level of communication. It made so many things so much easier. We were no longer just working and doing our jobs; we began to work with a purpose, and that was exciting. People actually talked about our pillars and keeping them in place. Honestly, in a very short time we worked better cross-functionally, had tighter integration between departments and coordinated our efforts, and everyone took ownership of their roles. For me, it was both exciting and interesting to see it happen."

The staff at Essentia began to live their mission, and the company changed. I was not certain they knew exactly who they were or what they were about when I arrived, but within those first three months, we all sensed the transformation that was underway. I began our regular town hall meetings with a discussion of the pillars we had established together for the company. What were we doing to advance each one of them? Were we using our individual voices to make the company stronger and better and more competitive? What did I suck at? What could the company do better? My own personal pillars, which I had long used to guide my life, were faith, family, other people, and business. I found that they aligned nicely with my new employer and the people I had been tasked with leading. I spoke of the Summit Mindset as a way of being, not just achieving, and I hoped we would all continue evolving as a team.

The greatest change for our staff showed up in improved communications. I always tell people that communicating is both the easiest and the hardest task to do, in our personal lives and in business. Failing at this one can ruin relationships or destroy businesses. Proper and effective communication involves being focused and intentional. Good and honest communication almost always improves a situation. I noticed at Essentia that we were speaking more clearly and regularly as a team, and as internal communications improved our operations, our external outreach to vendors and distributors also enhanced our reputation and improved marketing and brand image for the company. Whether the team realized it or not, we were beginning to live the Summit Mindset. During this time, I was most proud watching how we became a culture that said what we did and did what we said. Even as the entire country seemed stalled by powerful crises related to a virus and racial anger that our nation felt almost helpless to control, in our little bottled water company, we were making progress.

When people ask me about my statement that communicating is one of the hardest tasks to do, I can point them to several examples of bungling the job. The considerations must be made carefully regarding message and audience, and even the medium of delivery when sending a group message. In an enterprise, there is a risk of being too distant and corporate from employees or you might even fumble the entire outreach with poor language on a sensitive subject. In fact, the larger a company becomes, the more critical the communications platform is, and the understanding of the media and tools used to carry messages must keep pace, whether those messages are to shareholders, investors, customers, or employees.

We can't really know what Vishal Garg, the CEO of Better.com, was thinking when he had to make a difficult decision about reducing staffing because of economic conditions. His company, a growing online mortgage provider, was hit hard by the pandemic and a housing slowdown. Garg's team identified the operations that needed to be downsized and then either he or his corporate communications team chose a Zoom call to let nine hundred employees know they were to be released from employment. Only those included in the reduction in force decision were emailed with a link to join the Zoom. Because not everyone got an invitation, rumor and speculation spread throughout the company regarding the purpose of the video meeting. Garg gave his employees the bad news via the video conference that they were being fired because uncontrollable economic conditions had necessitated downsizing.

The convenience of the group video might have worked for the CEO's schedule and a staff working from home, but it seemed to the recipients to be an insensitive approach and bad form for the boss. Maybe Garg and his team did not have the awareness and experience to understand how business culture has changed; employees are far more than just a business asset. There are certain skills and techniques that just aren't taught in business schools and are better learned on the factory floor or its digital equivalent. The workforce of Better.com took to social media networks and emails and chat rooms to attack the company's leadership for poorly handling life-altering events for people who had played a role in the company's success. The stock took a hit, and the brand image was also harmed. Garg took some time off.

Garg and his leadership team failed to follow a corporate best practice: always have a culture in place to be transparent and authentic. Garg ought to have called a town hall meeting with all the employees to explain the decisions he would be making to downsize the organization. This would have also allowed him to personally thank all the employees for their hard work and demonstrate empathy for those being released, and maybe assure them they would be first in line to be rehired when the economy improved. People need to be treated with respect, not numbers on a spreadsheet.

External communications can be even more important than internal for a company, especially during a crisis. The right tactics can make the difference between a continued existence or a permanent disappearance from the marketplace. When a global leader in orthopedic implant devices failed to recognize the importance of transparent communications during a crisis, the company paid a dear price. The assembly line used to manufacture knee and hip implants had accidentally been polluted by an oil, and unknown to technicians, it was coating parts of the implants. When they were finally delivered to surgeons for hip and knee replacement procedures, postoperative recuperating patients began to reject their implants. Bone would not attach because of the coating of a foreign substance. Hundreds of people around the world endured more than one operation to replace their joints before the contamination was identified.

No one was surprised when aggrieved medical patients began to take their complaints public and talk to reporters and, of course, lawyers. Doctors were also open about what they were encountering. The shocking fact, though, was that the company refused to speak publicly about the problem. Executives in the C-suite knew they were dealing with a serious brand issue since they had hired a global public relations firm, but they ignored advice about transparency. The company began to develop a reputation of being secretive, and doctors started to back away from the use of their products. The best strategy would have been to publicly acknowledge what had happened and explain how it had been corrected and why the company's products were safer and better after the improvements in the manufacturing process. Finally, public contrition and a full apology might have reduced some consumer anger and financial liability.

None of that happened, though. While network TV news crews and global print reporters camped outside the corporate offices, leadership maintained it had no obligation to speak about a company's controversies. There were no rules, of course, but a bit of common sense might have averted the impending disaster. The patients grew impatient for answers, and lawsuits started piling up at US courthouses and in legal jurisdictions around the world. Eventually, the company, which had improved its processes and products but spoke little about the advancements, fired its CEO. The obstructionist strategy toward information and communications was costly, and legal settlements reached more than a billion dollars. Corporate assets were sold off to other similar industries, and a business that was previously a leading global brand in human joint implants simply ceased to exist.

There is a reasonable question to be asked about why a company should air out its problems in the public. Couldn't the implant manufacturer simply send out communications internally to employees and shareholders instead of exposing itself to public criticism in the media? They could, of course, and that's generally what the implant device company did, but the only accomplishment was the demise of the business. The unavoidable certainty was that the information was going to get out and it would make the firm look secretive, apply a negative connotation to the entire problem, and lack any input or perspective from management. Reporters were prompted to write stories that involved interviews with patients and doctors who were struggling to find out what exactly had happened and, worse, they spoke with third-party experts who indulged in speculation that was more harmful than any version of the truth. A crisis is not a time to *turtle up*.

Nothing is more critical in the Summit Mindset program than communicating, transparently and honestly. Processes fall apart without proper communication between individuals in personal relationships, and between coworkers, but especially when dealing with outside stakeholders like customers and vendors and the people who market your products. Transparency might have saved the implant company. Yes, there would have still been lawsuits to settle and huge write-downs on their books, but I think the brand would have recovered. People wanted to trust their products because they had trusted and used them in the past without complications. Admitting a mistake, apologizing, and correcting it could have given the company a chance at a comeback instead of bankruptcy.

By contrast, in 1982, Johnson & Johnson, the parent company of McNeil Consumer Products, the manufacturers of Tylenol pain relief medicine, handled the Tylenol tampering crisis well. In a case that has never been solved, someone tampered with Tylenol and placed cyanide inside of the gel caps before resealing bottles and secretly returning them to store shelves for sale. Before this criminal act, Tylenol owned 37 percent of the pain relief market share and outsold its combined four closest competitors. Unfortunately, the cyanide-laced capsules caused the deaths of seven people, and suddenly a trusted corporation had to explain itself to the world and why its popular product was killing people. Leadership, in Tylenol's case, did not hesitate to be forthcoming.

Johnson & Johnson spent money on public relations and advertising to set up toll-free numbers for the public and the media to get information on the investigation into who had contaminated Tylenol and what was being done to resolve the problems. The company quickly established a simple strategy of protecting the public first and, second, saving its valuable product, if possible. Initial coverage of the package tampering was negative because the media was unaware of the fact that persons unknown had injected capsules with deadly cyanide. An assumption was made that the company was at fault. Dedication to transparency and communication, though, is what saved it from total collapse. Executives set up live satellite TV feeds to New York City to openly answer questions, and that uplink technology enabled the story about what had happened to get national exposure. Every TV and radio station and broadcast network in America was able to access that audio and video feed. Eventually clipping services, which track the exposure and reach of news stories, indicated there had been more than 125,000 headlines related to the Tylenol tragedy, which was later described to be the second most reported story in history since the assassination of President John Fitzgerald Kennedy in 1963.

Tylenol had acted quickly to order a national recall of all its product on shelves and endured losses in the millions. The company was, however, able to use a sympathy and forgiveness strategy very effectively because it had become a victim of external forces. Johnson & Johnson provided money and counseling help to families that had suffered loss. The company then changed packaging to use a triple seal on bottles and focused its messaging on public safety. Using their CEO to deal directly with journalists and not practice avoidance also eliminated an adversarial relationship, and a public apology calmed the consumer to the point of forgiveness. The contamination of the capsules came to be considered one of the first acts of terrorism recognized by Americans, but Tylenol had so effectively managed the crisis that it not only survived, but it also returned to prominence on the shelf. Tylenol recovered its entire market share that it held prior to the loss of life.

I can't imagine dealing with the type of adversity that confronted Johnson & Johnson and its Tylenol team, but I know that preparation and teamwork are what make for a successful business. Their company also made a smart move by placing people above profits. Remember that the first part of their plan was the safety of the public, which also meant their consumers. Saving the product was secondary, but by choosing people first, they also kept Tylenol and the company in the marketplace. Executives and leadership worked up a plan and then executed against it, remaining diligent throughout the crisis, keeping employees and stakeholders informed of their efforts. This is why the Tylenol tragedy and how it was handled is still taught in business and communications classes four decades after the pain reliever was contaminated with cyanide.

We were dealing with uncontrollable external forces at Essentia too, as the crises hurting our country were having a discernible impact on the company's workforce. We had made a statement about racial injustices with outreach to African American groups and donations in the wake of the George Floyd incident, but the pandemic had infiltrated the lives of every employee because they were all working from home. I did not think that we would get the needed level of productivity and engagement to grow when interactions were limited to technology and when parents in our employ were dealing with children in the household because schools were closed. How was I going to get our entire team to work together to deal with an adversity that appeared to have no foreseeable end? Every organization I have worked in has shown me that adversity brings out the best and the worst in people, and I wanted to assure that we had the best.

A moment came when I realized I needed to demonstrate to our team that I didn't just talk the talk but that I walked the walk as well. I am aware there are critics who have suggested I sound like a walking self-help book, but I've shown consistently that my recipe for happiness and success in life and business can work. At an early town hall meeting, Essentia staff had indicated that one of our four strategic pillars was to put *people first*, and that aligned with my personal pillars. I think life is better and we are happier when we consider others and how we can help make life better for our communities and families and friends. I concluded I needed to prove to our employees that the company and I lived our strategic pillars, and that the mission and values were real to me and not simply words in frames hanging in hallways and offices.

Working from home may sound easy, but when everyone else is in the house trying to manage their tasks, things can get complicated. School-age children learning from teachers on video screens and moving through rooms while parents are doing their jobs remotely can make work and home life difficult, especially if the household budget does not allow for sitters and if parents must divide their work schedules. We came up with a plan to make dealing with the pandemic easier for Essentia's employees by providing a one-time cash payment to families with children sixteen years or under living at home. We decided to give them $5,000 to use any way they thought best, which, in most cases, involved computer technology or childcare services to reduce anxieties for parents. The company invested a total of $500,000 in our employees and their children. The most important pillar we had chosen as a company was *people first*, and our leadership team had just exhibited our determination to live and work by that principle and inspire our employees.

And that's exactly what happened.

Essentia's chief financial officer Chuck Czerkawski watched the transition daily when dealing with colleagues from home. They were already beginning to adopt parts of the Summit Mindset, but the company's gesture to help their families made it manifest in their daily lives. Czerkawski realized how powerful this demonstration of caring was when our employees got back in the building.

"There was really this impact on behavior and a buy-in that was almost mind boggling to me," he said. "People had reset their own expectations to a higher level and had inspired, I think, their own thought processes to live beyond themselves. There was this structural recalibration of our values, and it was participatory because everyone realized they had a voice in the process. We weren't significantly different than we had been on paper before, but our methods of communication were changing and working better, and we all took part. Really, there was complete buy-in and with a lot of latitude to participate but also accountability. It just worked, and that all happened within a month. Everyone was thinking, this is where the company is going to pivot, and we are actually going to get to the summit."

Companies need to stop and take notice when people have personal adversity. Often, employees are embarrassed by work-life challenges, and management needs to send a message of support, which is what we tried to do during the pandemic. Dignity for the workforce begins in the boardroom and the C-suite and lets people know the company is on their side when they need help. High-performing organizations of any kind can lose their humanity, becoming cutthroat and not recognizing the value of intangibles like happy people doing work they enjoy. When teams are galvanized around a common goal, giving someone time off to deal with personal issues or work away from the office ought to be of no consequence to the company's performance but of great value to the employee.

The Summit Mindset, I saw, was proving itself again in a business environment, and we were just getting started.

Exercises:

- **Strategic Pillars:** People need pillars for guidance in life and business just like organizations. Many will identify more than just four because we humans are complex creatures. But try to select the four most important to create the cornerstones to keep you or your company pointed at your North Star. Do you have an inherent belief in the goodness of people? Do you believe businesses can change the world for the better and not just make profits? Does your faith convince you there is a greater plan unfolding and you are playing a part? Will you weigh every decision you make on how it impacts other people before you follow through with plans? Are you convinced hard work and dedication solve all or most problems of life and work? When you have identified the four pillars that you know are a part of who you are and your daily life, consider them set in place and point them at your North Star.

Ask yourself every day, "What do I suck at? Where do I need to adjust?" Remain constructively dissatisfied, review the tape, recalibrate, and reset. It makes for happier humans.

- **Messaging:** Do you have a business that sells a product or a service? If so, have you ever thought about messages for what you are selling? Think of the four declarative statements you would make to best describe what your company offers. Write them down and refine what you want people to understand about your products or services. Now write secondary messages for each one of those primary, or key, messages. What's the next important statement to accompany your primary messages? Following are sample primary and secondary messages: *Primary: We are the best fence company in the entire state. Secondary: All our fences are made of rust-proofed iron.* Every person and business needs a primary and secondary message set. It is much like a North Star and gives us a framework for thinking of ourselves or our company and where we are going. Think of yourself as a business or a product. What are the four most important characteristics a potential employer or customer might need to know about you? Write down a half dozen that you think are essential to your character and abilities. Try reducing that number by half. Media trainers and communications experts teach that audiences can only process three messages, and they only remember one. What is the most important message you want remembered about you when communicating about a job or trying to land a client or customer? Make it your top-line message, and reinforce it with the other two. Your audience will recall only the one you've emphasized as central to who you are. Let your language leave no doubt about that. How would you have communicated, if you were the CEO of Better.com, the news to nine hundred people that they were being released? Was there a better way? Did the people who were being told overreact to the news? Write out the message you would have delivered to the loyal employees who were being let go.

CHAPTER FOUR

BE UNCONQUERABLE

It took me seventeen years and 114 days to become an overnight sensation.

—LIONEL MESSI, ARGENTINE SOCCER HERO

There is a story about legendary professional golfer Sam Snead that says he didn't have to work very hard to develop his swing. His friends often said that the first time "Slammin' Sam" addressed a teed-up ball and hit it, his swing was almost exactly as it was when his historic career came to an end. Jack Nicklaus described it as "the most fluid and elegant movement ever seen on a golf course." Snead must have been a natural because he kept playing and winning throughout his long life. At age sixty-seven, he shot two rounds in the Quad Cities of Iowa with scores lower than his age, the first time that had ever happened in the history of the Professional Golf Association, and when he won a tournament at age fifty-two, he became the oldest pro to ever accomplish that feat.

I'm not a golfer, but I have great appreciation for anything well done. Except maybe for Mr. Snead, most of us require commitment and hard work to achieve our goals. You can't simply decide you want to be a professional athlete and then show up at the ballpark, and surgeons don't just walk into the OR and begin performing heart surgery. Everything is about a process, which is driven by determination and dedication. You need a vision and a plan, and then you must put in the work, each day taking what I call *smart actions*, and accumulating the small brush strokes that will one day fill your life's canvas with the beautiful art you long ago imagined.

Because I enjoy reading, I often find myself thinking about what goes into creating a memorable book and how the author managed to complete such a complex undertaking. Even though Ernest Hemingway, one of America's greatest writers, was known almost as much for some of his bad habits as he was his stories, he never failed to do the daily task of getting new words down on paper. As a young man in France after World War I, he was known to stay out late partying, going to the horse tracks, and indulging in the feast of food and drink and culture that Paris had to offer. Hemingway was, however, up every morning at the same time, 6:00 a.m., drank a glass of water, wiped his face with a cold, wet cloth, and put his yellow legal pad on a window ledge. He stood there staring out at the alley and writing with his pencil for six or seven hours, seven days a week, until he had created the characters and events that turned his novels into great American literature. His habits created his greatness. Ours can change our lives, too.

The practice of developing habits and consistency of effort can, and has, changed the world, and not only the lives of individuals and organizations. When Marie Curie moved to Paris from Poland, she lived on pennies in a lonely research garret. Her meals consisted mostly of tea, bread, and butter, but every night she went to her makeshift laboratory and worked long hours on her research. When she met her future husband, Pierre, they began to share their struggle and, through consistent experimentation and theoretical extrapolation, discovered polonium and radium, which were two previously unknown elements. They then identified radiation and a property Curie described as "radioactivity." For their combined efforts, they shared a Nobel Prize in Physics in

1903. The birth of her two daughters and the sudden death of her husband did not slow Curie's intense research or her determination and curiosity to better understand nature. She became the first woman in history to receive a title of professor and to teach at the Sorbonne University in Paris and was awarded a second Nobel Prize for her isolation of pure radium, an accomplishment that began to transform medical treatments. Curie was the first woman to win a Nobel and the first individual to twice be given science's highest honor. Her work continues to influence modern medicine and research.

My analysis has shown me that habits turn into behavior, and if the habits are not positive, the outcomes will be detrimental. When I talk about the Summit Mindset, I remind my teams that one of the most important factors of achievement, as I've previously indicated, is *doing the reps*. The phrase is most closely associated with weightlifting and physical training, doing repetitions of lifting or pushing with different weights to increase muscle power. Repetitions of certain exercises create muscular growth when combined with proper nutrition, which enables the lifting of greater weight and the resulting increase in physical power. But the first day of lifting changes nothing other than to probably create next-day muscle soreness. Over time, a dedicated training program and attention to the details of exertion and recovery and food will transform most anyone's physique. The same determination to do the reps of a different type can alter careers and business results.

Failures in life often are the result of a confusion between intention and action—intending to do something is not the same as doing it. A New Year's resolution to get fit, lose weight, or find a new job are all admirable goals, but without a plan for achievement, they are just words. Taking steps daily, even small ones, is how we achieve. Action and application are the keys to success, and I believe it is essential to take a daily inventory on where we stand with our goals, what we have accomplished, what is in front of us, and what we have yet to do to arrive at our vision. Consistency turns into habits, and that transforms into performance for an organization or an individual. Doing your daily reps makes equity deposits in who you want to become and increases the value of your work to the business or organization. Our character also is strengthened for readiness and the inevitable confrontations with adversity that life delivers to almost everyone.

The Summit Mindset advises us to draw up an action plan and map out where we want to go as a person or a business. Establish your goal and then outline the major steps needed to reach achievement. Within each of those mileposts, other actions are required to progress. Mark those down too, and check them off as you move past each one toward the bigger idea. Make sure they are what you would consider *smart actions*, choices that move the project forward. I have used with success a technique referred to as a *parking lot*. The idea is to chart the various steps that are critical to success and then put them on a whiteboard that serves as a kind of holding area, the parking lot, for each of those elements. As those steps are completed, they are moved out of the parking lot as the project moves closer to being finished.

Visuals help when managing any project. I am a visual person. I always map out important undertakings. I put dates on the goals in the parking lot, and then our teams are maniacal about what they need to do to drive those markers out. I've seen organizations get lost on things they need to accomplish, and everyone ends up feeling like they are in orbit around the larger idea. White noise surrounds these kinds of efforts, and you must try to define tangible steps and timelines for achievement, otherwise what you are trying to get done will languish. The parking lot is a basic tool, but it keeps people moving and accountable. I always map out a path for important work, especially when it is collaborative, and we have discussions daily to hold ourselves accountable and figure out ways to make progress.

When I arrived at Essentia, the company had been developing the idea for a two-gallon box of water. The concept was a market differentiator and a potentially significant source of new revenue. Using recycled paper and reducing plastic consumption gave the box idea an environmental appeal, an increasingly popular characteristic among consumer products across the marketplace. Unfortunately, the project had been sitting in a queue for two and a half years without any real progress. We needed to map out how to execute the box project and then change our behavior, individually and organizationally, to get the new product into stores. Key factors were mapped out by the senior leadership team and put into the parking lot. These included the design and color of the box, marketing ideas and product messaging, finding a manufacturer for the boxes, competitive research, and analyses on pricing. Assignments were handed out, and we ran daily checks to make sure we were gathering useful data to implement the product and its launch.

The major issue with this product innovation was the manufacture of the two-gallon box. Essentia had no such facilities and we had to find a contractor with the capabilities to produce enough containers to meet market demand, which our research indicated would be strong. Team leaders were assigned to various needs for the box project, and we met almost daily to assess our progress and push tasks out of the parking lot into the completed category. But the manufacturing of the boxes with their interior plastic bladders to contain the water was our biggest challenge. The map we had lain out as a group was advancing nicely, though, and we were getting close to meeting a ninety-day challenge I had established for fulfilling the innovative idea.

To solve the manufacturing issue, we were not going to invest large amounts of capital to build our own assembly line. We had to approach an existing bottling company, one that might find revenue potential in having such capabilities. Eventually, we shared costs for the construction of a manufacturing process so we could get our new box to the market quickly. Work started on the line in April, and our first product was created in July, ready for sale. While much of the previous business conversation had concentrated on barriers to entry, we had turned our focus to solutions to entry in the market. Our team, when challenged and held accountable, executed against a plan that delivered innovation and environmental sensitivity, which (the following year) was honored by the industry for "Package of the Year."

This achievement was a result of achieving the mandates of the Summit Mindset. We did the reps, every day assessing where we were compared to where we wanted to be, and then we took smart actions to step toward our goals. Those small advances we made each day were also aligned with Essentia's pillars and kept us pointed toward our North Star of becoming the number one premium water on a global basis. We had planned, held ourselves accountable, executed against our defined goals, and succeeded. Sales and marketing hit the ground fast with outreach for the new box of water, which quickly landed space in big-box stores, turning the product into an important added source of innovation and revenue for the company.

The successful plan for the water box was developed through discussion, debate, and feedback on our ideas. We listened carefully to the input of team leaders and department experts, making certain that everyone understood their voice was valued in the process. There were, as might be expected in any large group, people who were dissatisfied with our strategy and the final shape of the plan, but we made sure they understood why certain decisions were made and the actions we intended to take to make the box a reality in the company's product line. Getting a large organization to listen is not a small task. People grow accustomed over long periods of time in a business to doing things a certain way, and getting them to put those failed habits aside and take the new approach is rarely easy. Open and honest communication and meaningful engagement tends to generate understanding and trust.

In business and our personal lives, I have long found the simplest way to achieve any goal is a consistent behavior. But that behavior must be built upon smart actions. Aristotle said, "We are what we repeatedly do," but I think there are also nuances to using habits to move through life. When we pass a certain milepost, our behaviors and actions might need to change, even if just slightly, to turn us in the direction of our next objective. Doing the same thing consistently is valuable only when it leads to an improvement. When conducting scientific research, inputs and data are changed when results are consistently repeated but don't yield the sought-after insights. I think our habits need to be recalibrated in a similar fashion. Let yourself move toward what is working, and readjust as necessary to point in the direction of your desired results. There's no more basic method of getting what you want out of life and business.

I also talk in the Summit Mindset about the importance of being constructively dissatisfied. I've made reference to this previously, but I think the details and logic that that notion is built upon are valuable for us as individuals. When you accomplish something, is it precisely what you wanted to achieve? Aren't you always wondering what you might have done better? Successful people are always trying to find ways to improve even as they are accomplishing their goals. There might be satisfaction in reaching a target, but did it turn out exactly as you wanted, or does it motivate you to push on to what might be even greater? Have you ever met a golfer who wasn't working on their swing? A golf swing is a metaphor in many ways for life and business. The slightest adjustments can send the ball off into the rough or straight and true down a fairway. My experience is, we need to constantly make those adjustments even as we fulfill our ambitions because the greatest achievers I've known tend to have an edge of dissatisfaction. An architect might consider her latest building to be a design that speaks to modern culture, but she can also walk away wondering if there should have been something in the structure that spoke to the history of its environment and the people who inhabit the local landscape. Dissatisfaction, used constructively, can be a powerful tool. Don't let it rob your joy of accomplishment, but keep it as an emotional asset to drive you to ever greater achievements. The next building that architect designs will likely have an increased sensitivity to all the elements of its surroundings.

The dissatisfaction of leaders is, in many ways, an even more important dynamic in business. During the two-gallon water box project, we all learned to use the Summit Mindset tactic of asking ourselves, "What do I stink at?" I consider that question one of its most critical elements. At our team meetings, I was the first to ask it of myself. This is a difficult thing to do because most of us are raised to think that stinking at things is a form of weakness; instead, it's about being human and growing. Especially in organizations, posing the question to ourselves as servant leaders is humanizing, and it becomes a strength. Growth is also a product of this self-examination. Reflecting on a mistake, sharing it with others, learning how to be a better leader or employee or person, has always seemed to me to be a great process for personal advancement. I taught myself to embrace the things I sucked at because it made me introspective and analytical, which also led to personal improvement. A persistence of effort grew out of that for me, and others, and I developed the habit of looking for *little nuggets* of experience or information that I might use to effect a positive change. If I had an idea to try a policy or tactic on a personal basis because I suspected it might improve my performance or add to my happiness, as an example, I then looked to how it might help the company. I also reconsidered practices that were institutionalized but might need rethinking, even when they were minor. The cumulative effect of these small adjustments was often significant both for the company and me.

These practices for leaders and staff employees helped us create a culture at Essentia that grew the company. Reaching out to the community after the death of George Floyd and offering the financial assistance to our employees during the pandemic made everyone working for us realize an engaged culture was to become a characteristic of our operations. My goal was to establish and reaffirm a set of values by which we could work and live. Through consistent behavior and actions, we were communicating to our group what we stood for as an organization and as people. Culture must be given life through stated common goals and a cause greater than ourselves, which in business and work is your North Star. I see culture as the galvanizing principle to drive forward the individual and the organization, and, at its best, as a vehicle for providing a higher purpose within the broader community.

There are numerous definitions for a positive business culture, and they encompass many different factors. Culture is more than just a Ping-Pong table and free beer in the break room, though such perks can be motivating for workers. Everybody wants to do their job in a fun environment, but culture cannot be developed at the cost of productivity; it needs to enhance company output and accomplishments. Employees also want positive feedback, not just negative criticisms. Management must develop trust with transparent communication and offer flexibility to employees. I think every organization needs to be supportive and helpful of people who are facing challenges in their private lives. This type of awareness and caring creates a bond within any group but especially employees, because people have come not to expect that in American business. All this will lead to a successful collaboration among staff who have shared goals and values; performance improves and their efforts become harmonious.

Developing a culture can be a complicated task, and a failure at the responsibility can be harmful to a business, regardless of its size. Two of the biggest companies in America continue to struggle with their cultural images. Even as it was going public, ride share giant Uber acknowledged its failure to get it right in a statement to potential investors.

"Our workplace culture and forward-leaning approach," a company statement read, "created significant operational and cultural challenges that have in the past harmed, and may in the future continue to harm, our business results and financial condition. A failure to rehabilitate our brand and reputation will cause our business to suffer."

To describe Uber's corporate culture as toxic almost understates the matter after a public blog post by Susan Fowler. The Uber engineer kept detailed records of sexual harassment and discrimination against women along with evidence of a management structure that refused to even recognize her claims as a problem. Fowler said early during her employment that her new team manager sent her a series of texts on a company chat service to explain he was in an open relationship with his girlfriend and was looking for women to have sex with. She took screenshots of what he had sent her and then took her concerns to HR, where she was told the man was a "high performer" and that, since this was his first offense, he deserved only a stern warning. She was also told to expect a negative review from that supervisor for reporting him, and there was nothing to be done about that unfairness, either. Fowler discovered, after talking with other women at Uber, the manager had been accused of sexual harassment several times and had avoided any kind of punishment.

Fowler's email is part of what prompted the *New York Times* to take a closer look at what Uber called its culture, and the problems were more manifest than what the former engineer had detailed.[1] In a long investigative piece published in the newspaper, employees were quoted who said that one supervisor used a homophobic slur during a loud confrontation in a meeting, an Uber manager grabbed a female coworker's breasts while attending a company retreat in Las Vegas, and another threatened to beat an underperforming employee's head in with a baseball bat. The newspaper also reported that Uber employees were using cocaine in the bathrooms of the hotel where the Las Vegas retreat was being held. Some of that might have been unsurprising given previous comments by Uber's cofounder and CEO, who once referred to his business as "Boob-er because of how easy it became for him to meet women."

The tone of every company's culture is established at the top and communicated to employees.

Uber's IPO turned out to be a failure of epic proportions thanks to bad publicity. In some ways, things only got worse over the next two years. A report on diversity showed that women held only 14 percent of leadership roles in the company, and Black and Latina women had 0 percent of those jobs. Men had 72 percent of management positions. Disclosures of that type of data contributed to Uber experiencing a $5.2 billion loss in one quarter during 2019. Uber went to work on issues of inclusion, equity, and diversity and publicly reported, not quite five years after the Fowler letter, that it had shown improvement in women and Blacks in leadership roles. The company said employment of racially underrepresented groups was up 4 percentage points and double that figure for leadership positions. Women in management in the US was supposedly up by just over 11 percent during the same period, and racially underrepresented groups working for the tech sections of Uber increased by 7.2 percentage points, according to the company's internal statistics.

But what went wrong with Uber's culture?

---

1   Maureen Dowd, "She's 26, and Brought Down Uber's CEO. What's Next," *The New York Times*, October 21, 2017.

I suspect they grew too fast. Growth of personnel, technology, and revenue ballooned with a speed that made it difficult to manage. Nobody in the C-suite or among senior leaders had much time to ponder ideas like culture and the kind of company Uber might become over time, or even in the short term. The founder did develop leadership principles, but this can be considered a different notion than culture. Offices around the globe were undoubtedly filled with people driven by ambition and opportunity, which is only good when it is aligned with other company goals and purposes. Otherwise, the culture becomes one of every man and woman out for themselves, constantly seeking an advantage that will earn them promotions and stock and accolades. Was there ever any time during the company's launch and speedy growth to think about the matter of culture? I know young entrepreneurs consider creating a work culture that is more relaxed and less pressured, but it is often hard to figure out where these companies are going or what is their larger vision.

Uber's attempt at a positive and defining culture began with mimicking Amazon. Founders developed fourteen core values that were derivative of the sixteen leadership principles of the global retail giant. Amazon's size required a set of standards to be communicated to managers and, if adhered to, could drive a strong cultural presence within the company. These guidelines included hiring and developing the best talent, being obsessed with the customer, insisting on the highest standards, having a bias for action with the clarification that "speed matters in business," earning trust, having a backbone to "disagree and commit," thinking big to learn and be curious, delivering results, and inventing and simplifying. Most important among the aspirations listed by Amazon was to "strive to be Earth's best employer." Even Amazon, which has the resources and the intellectual capital to accomplish almost any business ambition, has struggled with culture and especially that last edict to be the planet's best employer.

In its warehousing and packaging division, Amazon has suffered bad publicity and employee criticisms related to working conditions and pay. Problems began when a group of more than two hundred health care professionals conducted an investigation of warehouse operations and discovered that Amazon had "nearly double the national average of warehouse workplace injury," which the report said was caused by "chronic stress from the workload and work quota system" and combined with a "risk of contracting chronic and infectious disease due to lack of restroom access and inadequate COVID-19 protections."[2] Amazon's turnover rate for employees is a huge negative for the company, with the typical worker remaining on their payroll for less than a year. Whatever comforts and standards were being experienced by management, apparently they were not being realized by employees at the level where products are processed and delivered. Workers were unhappy, and that is always a prescription for trouble.

How has the company responded? According to the National Labor Relations Board, when employees at warehouses in Alabama began a movement to sign up people to join a union at Amazon, the management used what were described as intense intimidation tactics that were illegal and "flagrant unfair labor practices." The company defeated, at least temporarily, the union organizing effort in Alabama, where there is not a strong union presence in general, with just over 6 percent of workers having union memberships. In New York, however, on April Fools' Day 2022, the employees at Amazon's huge warehouse on Staten Island voted overwhelmingly to form a union. The story in the *New York Times* said, "No union victory is bigger than the first win in the United States at Amazon, which many union leaders regard as an existential threat to labor standards across the economy because it touches so many industries and frequently dominates them."[3] The pandemic and a nationwide labor shortage are breathing life into the renewed union movement in the US, but it also appears to be driven by failure in business cultures.

---

2   "The Public Health Crisis Hidden in Amazon Warehouses," The Human Impact Project, January 2021, https://humanimpact.org/hipprojects/amazon/.

3   Karen Weise and Noam Scheiber, "Amazon Workers on Staten Island Vote to Unionize in Landmark Win for Labor," *The New York Times*, April 1, 2022, https://www.nytimes.com/2022/04/01/technology/amazon-union-staten-island.html.

There are some reasonable questions to ask about culture at Amazon and Uber, and they might be instructive since both companies were founded on essentially the same principles. I've wondered if management lived the culture daily and modeled it for managers and workers to see it in action and believe in its implementation. Yes, I think it likely that both global conglomerates grew so quickly they lost sight of who they were and what they believed in at the beginning, or maybe those lofty words were nothing more than inscriptions for marketing collaterals or quotes for email footers. At the heart of every business culture is caring for people who work for you. Media reports of what happened inside of Amazon and Uber can certainly lead outsiders to think the desire for shareholder value and growing revenues were more important than making certain they were building a great place to work. Through advertising, Amazon touted increasing wages for warehouse workers, but it still appears to be less than what is considered a livable wage in most American cities.

While Uber shifted focus to inclusion and diversity and has made progress, there is still no real indication of sweeping cultural changes or improvements.

A few of Amazon's principles fit well with what I've developed through years of working on the Summit Mindset. Although they would not have characterized it as such, the company's North Star, "to be Earth's best employer," is powerful and ambitious. Their leadership principles, though, tend to be concentrated on matters of revenue and growth rather than the people in their employ. The company does seem to understand the responsibilities that come with its scale and size and says, "We must begin each day with a determination to make better, do better, and be better for our customers, our employees, our partners, and the world at large." This is soaring ideology, to be certain, but it falls apart when warehouse workers say their bathroom usage is restricted and rest breaks are so infrequent that they are experiencing physical pain and deteriorating health.

Little is more essential to life and business than adaptation. It's possible these two giants of American enterprise didn't adjust. Different departments within large companies can become so big they begin to act as individual businesses, and what was once a well-integrated operation turns into a series of silos, often interacting with other units in a disconnected fashion. I've seen this happen in companies that brought me on board to effect change. My standard has always been to keep an eye on external developments and monitor marketplace conditions with great diligence. I think it is important for companies of all sizes to have the information they need to evolve and shift, which allows them to respond to the moment and condition of their times. There is no other way to stay true to their stated values.

What I hope that people will learn from the Summit Mindset is that caring can facilitate greater ambition and hard work. When we gave each employee $5,000 if they had children sixteen years or younger at home, we allowed them to use the money however they needed, but most bought computers for home learning or paid for childcare to enable them to continue their jobs while stuck at home during the pandemic. I think this decision by our leadership team helped the company coalesce in a difficult time and become part of our larger effort with a connection they had probably not anticipated.

Kazumi Mechling, who was the head of our corporate communications team, had a solid reputation in public relations and had dealt with the good and bad of many corporations. She holds culture and caring for workers in high regard.

"I think what we are talking about is love," she said. "You just don't see a lot of businesses being able to actually love and care about the people they work with. Isn't it strange we can have all these courses on harassment but none about just caring for your coworkers? Especially during the pandemic, people were just so isolated and did not feel cared about. But we developed a sense of balance with the Summit Mindset, honestly, and by caring about our people we were able to inspire them to go the distance to make the company excel and win for everyone. The $5,000 gift to each of our families was a clear indication we were serious, and it really helped the company as much as it did our employees who were struggling through the work-from-home problems."

A frequent honoree in annual lists of best places to work for is an online educational platform you may not have heard of called Chegg. They provide learning software for students in high school through college and consistently get rave reviews from their employees. Their focus on happy staffers was even more critical during the pandemic. The company immediately recognized childcare challenges for home-bound Chegg staffers and offered a $500-a-month stipend along with summer coding camps for employees' school-aged children, as well as vacation music and art camps for preschoolers. The company offered free sessions with mental health professionals for its team members. Management organized fitness and yoga online sessions for staff during times when the pandemic made work increasingly sedentary, and everyone got the week off work before July Fourth. Chegg specifically asked all employees to limit emails so that people could truly enjoy time for themselves. During summer months, everyone had Fridays off, and as fall arrived, the company transitioned to "no meetings Fridays."

Obviously, this is a company anyone would like to work for. Management already had a stellar reputation in the educational community and beyond as being employee-focused, but Chegg was even more astute at adjusting as the pandemic changed their circumstances. According to multiple reviews on sites like Glassdoor, there is almost no complaint about the work environment at Chegg, and even the pay is well above its industry standards. Companies that look inward, care about employees, and analyze what can be done to make them happy and productive experience positive business results and a motivated workforce. Enterprises have become so focused on the well-being of employees that top human resources executives in organizations are now referred to as CPOs, or chief people officers.

A positive trend has occurred as companies increase their attention on the communities where they live and work. Reputable businesses get involved in the cities and towns where they are based, and they participate in philanthropic and outreach activities. This idea is known as Corporate Social Responsibility (CSR), and enterprise-level companies employ CSR officers to drive positive engagement with the community by initiating fund-raising challenges, volunteering staff for important social projects, creating programs to lift the disadvantaged, and even establishing sustaining foundations. Numerous services have been spawned to create platforms that enable businesses to manage their CSR efforts. These often allow employees to select charities to donate to and have specific amounts deducted from their pay. Employees are encouraged to identify and promote local philanthropies, organizations to volunteer with, and humanitarian projects to join. Empowering your workers to make a difference for good is as critical as giving them the tools to accomplish their jobs inside your business.

CSR isn't just good for your city or state, either; it's also good for your company. When people meet your employees on charitable projects, it reflects positively on your brand. As a company's profile increases in social giving and volunteering, the brand image of that business and its products and services is strengthened. There is also evidence that customers are generally willing to pay more for products from socially responsible brands. I'd also point out, having been an executive at several enterprises that were committed to CSR, it's easier to attract and keep top talent because the best people always want to work for companies committed to improving the world. My experience has also shown me that socially responsible companies are more attractive to investors, who tend to be the kind of people I want putting money and advice into the companies where I work. I can't imagine a business being broadly successful without engaging in good works within and beyond its communities. One of the enduring mantras of my Summit Mindset has always been, "It's never about one of us. It's always about all of us." Corporate Social Responsibility is a demonstration of that belief.

A culture of caring isn't only about business, though. It's about heart as well. If you and your staff were only helping others to make more money and make your company look good, your charitable acts would be vain and hollow, serving the wrong purpose of profit. I don't recall ever meeting someone who has helped another in need who hasn't come through the experience feeling happier for their act of kindness. Doing for others fulfills us in a manner little else in life can. I've always thought that if you lined up every person on the planet and asked them what they wanted, their responses would almost universally be that they hoped to have happiness in their lives. That's what we all pursue. But as I've said, it begins with defining what happiness means to you. Too often, people see money as the solution to unhappiness. But we know it is not, because many of the most miserable souls on our planet, whose public behavior and practices betray their character, are often among the wealthiest.

I didn't have to spend much time trying to figure out my personal happiness. The idea of giving and doing for others has always brought me a sense of purpose. My pursuit of that purpose is what has given me happiness. I don't think there is anything that I feel more deeply than the joy that comes from, figuratively and literally, holding a door open for others. Happiness is more than just an emotional state, though. The pursuit of doing good, helping, and using those efforts to feed your personal spirit will also enhance your energy toward life and work. There is nothing esoteric or philosophical about our need to give back; it is a characteristic, I believe, of almost everyone. To make a positive impact on the lives of others, as well as our own, we need to cultivate what already exists in our hearts. A business must acquire these characteristics, and with the right kind of leadership, that goal can be achieved. The company will find its productivity and workforce transformed.

We also rarely think of such things during our workaday lives, but our actions and those of our businesses create legacies. Even small kindnesses affect how we will be remembered and any positive influence we leave behind. I feel that a life well lived, or a business operated by the precepts of the Summit Mindset, will create a meaningful legacy that can have enduring influence. This evolves from real humility and honesty. Every action we take creates a ripple effect, which can become a wave that changes countless lives. Staying in pursuit of such a dream can deliver us happiness while we are here and influence those around us by modeling behavior that makes a difference in the lives of others.

Isn't that worth trying?

Exercises:

- **Create a Culture:** Define your business principles. Ask yourself the basic question of what you want your culture to be. How will the characteristics of that culture contribute to the work-life balance of your employees? Remember, your goal should be to empower the members of your team to be their best on the job and at home. Try to accomplish the important task of designing a culture that puts people first. Plan for regularly reexamining your culture and its benefits to the company and employees.

- **Plan for Happiness:** What does happiness mean to you personally? Is there a specific way you inject happiness into your craft or business that also works in your personal life? After you have defined what happiness is for you, review the idea relentlessly in your work culture and personal life. Constantly talk with teammates about what needs to change or improve. Remember, being constructively dissatisfied keeps us all growth-minded. Talk with your teammates about what needs to change. Have you been happy even when you were struggling to make an income and pay your bills? If so, do you remember what brought you happiness during those tough times? Was it friends or family? Make a list of the activities you enjoy, and determine what steps you need to take to do them often. On your list, what do you identify as a material thing, and what is an event or accomplishment? Which feels more important? Let that guide you toward your happiness.

CHAPTER FIVE

OVERCOMING ADVERSITY

If you're going through hell, keep going.

—FDR

There is an old cliché we've all heard: the only two certainties in life are death and taxes. While those are guaranteed to be a part of everyone's experience, there is one other dynamic that is sure to deliver trouble. Almost everyone who ever draws a breath, no matter how gifted you are financially or physically, will deal with adversity. We can all expect inevitable problems with either our health, money, careers, broken hearts, or the pain that comes with making bad choices. Adversity cannot be avoided. What distinguishes us from one another is how we manage hardship—whether we take control or surrender to a bad situation.

The challenge is to not let difficult circumstances break us. The goal instead is to use them for learning and to make ourselves stronger. But it's sometimes easier to talk about an outcome than it is to achieve. Slogans don't mean much when you have lost your job and there's no money in the bank to pay the rent or buy groceries, and our thoughts turn not to strength but to survival. But I believe we are defined by how we manage our challenges and not what happens to us that we cannot control. Writer Ernest Hemingway, in a letter to his friend and fellow novelist F. Scott Fitzgerald, offered some simple advice on how to deal with Fitzgerald's failures in his personal life.

"Use the hurt, Scott," Hemingway wrote, implying that his stories would be more acute and alive if they were informed by his suffering.

Pain and discomfort, social or physical, are the source of much of history's greatest art, but most of us will not be known to the world as great musicians and we will not sculpt fine statues, nor will we paint masterpieces that live through the ages. We do, however, need to get through our hard times and learn how to use them to advance our lives and become better prepared to help others. The Summit Mindset acknowledges that adversity and challenges will keep coming, and at times they will feel overwhelming; the thought of surrender may enter your mind. We must accept that we do not have the power to control all the factors that will affect our lives, but I believe we can manage them by anticipating change and leaning into our difficulties as they arise. When we accept that adversity is central to life, we learn how to deal with it and how to prevent it from diminishing us and, instead, gain the confidence and experience to go on better prepared for whatever is next.

Dealing with adversity is also about context and perspective. There is an ancient Persian proverb that says, "I cried because I had no shoes until I saw a man without any feet." It's true that what I might consider adversity could be inconsequential to another person. There are those who would scoff at my discomfort and consider it a walk in a lovely park. That point of view, though, should not ignore the fact that I am suffering greatly and feeling pain from my set of circumstances. I have a friend who was raised by a single mother who had given birth to six children, dealt with her husband's violence and mental illness, adjusted to a new country as a seventeen-year-old immigrant with a baby, worked sixteen-hour days on her feet as a waitress to pay the bills, survived cancer, and started and lost a business that she had hoped would make things easier for her family. Regardless, my friend told me, well into her eighties, his mother was dismissive of all that she had overcome and reminded everyone there was a world full of people who had had it much worse.

How do you prepare for that kind of adversity? I'm not sure you can. These were the consequences of his mother's choices when she was a teenager. She fell in love with an American soldier, got pregnant, and left her island home. She could not know or be prepared for the decades of hardships to follow, but there are ways you can be ready for dealing with tough times or even lesser difficulties. In the Summit Mindset, I talk about the importance of building a foundation for your life using the four pillars. When you have established the pillars that point you toward the North Star you are seeking, you will have strength and the tools to withstand the challenges you confront. One of your pillars might be more relevant than another because your adversity is related to your career and profession, and you are surrounded by supportive colleagues who are interested in your success. They understand and offer counsel and guidance to sustain you through the mess, whether it is getting released because the company has economic issues, or maybe getting passed over for a promotion for which you were the logical choice. Passing through adversity of that nature is considerably more doable with career support even if one or more of your other pillars is not as viable at that point in your life.

A by-product of managing adversity is resilience. We become more capable of dealing with a variety of issues and know that we can handle hard times and bounce back, hopefully wiser from the experience and tempered with more confidence. The resilience we acquire is profoundly important for how we see ourselves and our capabilities. In fact, I view it as an essential characteristic for improving the human condition. People climbing to the summit can expect the climate to change, sometimes dramatically, but if they are ready for the harsh weather and uncomfortable conditions, they are likely to continue their ascent toward their North Star. A real mountaineer might carry extra food and water, insulated sleeping bags, and tents to protect them from the cold. Your protection is different and comes from confidence, experience, and psychological preparation, and the assurance that your four pillars will get you through the most complicated of life's problems.

Adversity that teaches resilience also comes from awareness. We spend too much of our energy and intellect trying to build a perfect life. We would be better prepared if we accepted the fact that life is not intended to be perfect, whatever our definition of perfect is. We are all going to struggle, so we must be aware of our strengths and weaknesses to prepare for inevitable problems. I know that having a positive attitude and being grateful for the sheer joy of just living is not an answer to dealing with a debilitating disease or recovering from a natural disaster, but I also believe that how you think will inform how you act in the wake of tragedy. The mind is very much a computer, and the data that goes in will show up in the data that comes out. "Garbage in, garbage out" is what programmers have always said. Put the best information and personal perspective that you can into your brain. Do not allow yourself to be swept away by negativity. We can accept defeat and live a diminished life—or we hold tight to our dreams and live in a manner that shows the world we understand what a gift it is to be able to try, to fail, learn, and try again.

My experience with adversity occurred just as I felt everything in my family and career was coming together in a balance that was very fulfilling and hopeful for our future. I had landed a great role at the Quaker Oats Company and was working on business development for their Gatorade and Snapple brands. The opportunity was exciting, but it required regular commuting between Chicago and our home on the East Coast. I was only thirty-two years old at the time, fit and healthy, with the optimism of increasing success. During one of my routine flights home, I found myself sitting on the plane doubled over with abdominal pain. I had no idea what was happening, but I was terribly frightened. I assumed I had eaten spoiled food or had an infection.

My greatest concern, of course, was for my family—my wife and our three young children. The stomach cramps and pain were such that, before we landed, I decided to go directly to the hospital. The initial suspicion in the emergency room was that I had a form of stomach cancer, but an additional round of tests led to a diagnosis of stage four ulcerative colitis. An inflammatory bowel disease, it leads to internal bleeding of the large intestine, causing blood in the stool, a lack of appetite, chronic weight loss, and various degrees of pain. The causes are uncertain but are thought to be related to protein imbalances in the body and even the external environment. I only know that I lost twenty pounds over the next two months, had difficulty controlling my bowels, and dealt with constant bleeding.

The doctors began immediate treatment with a drug called Asacol and put me on a protocol of fourteen pills daily, which was the highest dosage recommended by the FDA. The list of potential side effects was as frightening as my symptoms: nausea, vomiting, constipation, joint and muscle pain, headaches, and upset stomach. Physicians managing my case at New York University suggested the removal of my colon, which would have meant a colostomy. I was young and disapproved of this course of action. I was determined to fight, confident my positive perspective was going to get me to the other side of my affliction. After twelve years on Asacol, my symptoms were gone, but it had taken the first two years before they had stopped being acute. During those dozen years, I was scoped every month, and I continue to get the procedure once a year. I have achieved total remission, I believe, because my mind was unwilling to surrender to my body. Obviously, great medical care and pharmaceuticals were essential to sustaining my health, but I am certain my mindset was as much a factor in my recovery as was the professional treatment.

I stopped working the great job I had at Quaker Oats to focus on my health. After six months of getting to a less acute and more manageable state with my ulcerative colitis, I was back in the market looking for work when a senior leader from Quaker Oats called and offered me an opportunity to return to the company, which I happily accepted. They had filled my previous role but provided me a job that was smaller in scope and involved less responsibility. I was grateful for the chance to rebuild my career. I began to feel reenergized and started concentrating on the path forward. I suspect there are millions of books that could be written about people who have successfully confronted greater adversity than mine. These individuals, who are quite often athletes, motivate and inspire with their performances. Many times, as I have watched great athletic accomplishments, I've thought that certain people are born with their own kind of steely confidence, a belief they can do anything they imagine. They have a vision of themselves as champions and fierce competitors and there is little that can be put in front of them to prevent them from living out those dreams. I think the rest of us, though, can learn their determination by living our personal Summit Mindsets.

Because I have been a runner most of my life, I have often taken my inspiration from endurance athletes who overcome long odds, and I was particularly amazed by a forty-six-year-old woman from Arizona: Jacky Hunt-Broersma, who lost her lower left leg to a rare cancer and still set a world record by running 104 marathons in 104 days. She can run thanks to a carbon-fiber prosthesis. The total miles Hunt-Broersma accumulated in her personal quest was 2,704, which was the equivalent of running from New York City to Mexico City, an astonishing achievement. When training, world-class professional marathoners often log one hundred miles a week. Hunt-Broersma, by comparison, ran just over 180 miles every week for fifteen consecutive weeks.

What we also find among people dealing with adversity is the desire to give back. Hunt-Broersma, as an example, wasn't just running to achieve monumental recognition. She knew her effort was certain to attract attention, and she used that to raise money for other differently abled runners trying to pay for prostheses. The blades used by amputee runners average about $10,000, and Hunt-Broersma got donations that totaled $67,000, with more money offered to her cause even after she had finished. Her mantra, she said, was, "I can do hard things," which seems a remarkable understatement. She often wears a T-shirt emblazoned with the statement "Strong comes in many forms."

Give some thought to how Hunt-Broersma refused to be defined by her physical difference. She used the adversity of an amputated lower leg and the disease that took it from her to enhance her focus and determination to achieve. Not only did she confront her physical difference but she also took on one of the biggest challenges in endurance sports by running all those marathons. Fully abled people consider competing in one marathon a major accomplishment. She did 104 in a row with a prosthesis. She has demonstrated the fortitude to tackle most anything that gets in her way, and she carries that with her as both an armor and a tool. She might falter at some point, but Hunt-Broersma has the resilience of a person who arose each morning to face a steep hill, and she got to the peak every day. There might not be a better example of the value of adversity to transform and the human spirit to endure, which I believe is an ember glowing inside each of us.

Psychologists and sociologists have spent a lot of time studying how people respond when aspects of their lives fall apart, but they have only in recent years begun to look at how we recover. A study in the *Journal of Personality and Social Psychology* found that through dealing with adversity, many people develop a greater understanding of hardship and are more prepared for it when it comes again, and it most assuredly will return in most lives.[4] The report acknowledges that bad experiences cause us to suffer from spiritual, physical, and mental pain and that, frequently, we fail to release the pain and end up eating junk food, skipping exercise, and generally allowing ourselves to slip into a state of disrepair and willful helplessness.

The authors conclude that suffering and recovering leads to resiliency because we are forced to reach out to our friends and family and realize we cannot overcome all our struggles without help. This backup plan can give us a sense that we are prepared and know how to respond when the skies, inevitably, will once more darken. We begin to develop the mental and physical resources to manage whatever happens in our lives.

---

4   Robert A. Emmons and Michael E. McCullough, "Counting Blessings versus Burdens: An Experimental Investigation of Gratitude and Subjective Well-Being in Daily Life," *Journal of Personality and Social Psychology* 4, no. 2 (2003): 377–389.

I do not mean to suggest that every crisis can be overcome with force of will and the proper attitude. The Summit Mindset, though, teaches us that preparation and a spirit of strength and useful experience will take us to a better place. However, there are great troubles that can cause even the most readied individuals to feel hopeless and without control. These emotions can also put stress on your network of professional communities, friends, and families. The best way through these times, I believe, is to use our mind, body, and spirit while also taking steps like engaging a therapist or spiritual advisor. Like the runner Jacky Hunt-Broersma, you might acknowledge your physical limitations but then decide to surpass what the experts expect of a person with your challenge and redefine "possible" for others in a similar situation. I think it is important to honor our own self-worth throughout our hardships and to never be afraid to turn to our support groups, meditation, relaxing hobbies, and even the simple act of allowing ourselves to rest.

The most important consideration, though, is to never quit. The climate on the way to the summit will always be changing, which means improvement is inevitable. The research in the report I mentioned earlier also indicated that we may, in fact, be harming ourselves when we try to avoid adversity. We might become risk-averse, which will almost certainly diminish our chances of achieving our dreams. Or we find a way to numb our pain rather than deal with it. Addictions are born from that approach. Instead, we need to realize that adversity can bring out the best in us and deliver life's greatest lessons. We almost always learn who are our true friends, but we can also come to understand that when we put in the effort to deal with hardships, we find resourcefulness and empowerment. Often, the instinctive response to trouble is to run away, but the evidence is that when we make that choice, it robs us of growth that comes from meeting adversity and moving on to our next set of positive experiences.

By managing adversity, we also win another battle in the war I have characterized as You versus You. We choose to do the hard thing—to improve situations and outcomes—rather than letting circumstances take control. The Summit Mindset teaches us to play offense in life, not to let life happen to us. If we want something, we need to take the necessary steps to acquire it, whether it is simply a career goal or an aspiration like a romantic trip or a vacation property or a new car or going to college. Waiting for the right circumstances and environment to act is not a strategy for achievement. The same is true regarding adversity. We often see negative scenarios developing and, instead of taking steps to prevent or divert them, we simply let them happen and hope they will go away on their own or someone else will take control. Playing offense in life puts our hands on the wheel, builds our confidence, and prepares us for the return of adversity. The You versus You conflict swings toward a positive victory, even if the adversity we've confronted becomes impossible to manage. We still tried, learned, did the honorable thing, and were improved by our effort. By getting through the tough time, you can also create habits to deal with problems and set down building blocks of character that will keep you strong when the skies again get cloudy.

There is no question that adversities are capable of immobilizing individuals and organizations. I have seen businesses become so focused on an adversity or difficult challenge that they get close to destroying themselves. The Summit Mindset always puts goals ahead of dealing with adversity. You are free to manage circumstances in a manner that keeps your enterprise moving toward a goal, regardless of the roadblock. What people lose sight of is, rain falls on everyone, and only those who are prepared with shelter can avoid getting wet. This is why anticipating adversity, whether personal or business, will become a competitive advantage. A situation can go bad in a second, and being prepared and willing to embrace these challenges can determine our ability to overcome. If we maintain our concentration on goals, short and long term, we are able to envision opportunities that are hidden within the unexpected complications that arrive in the middle of an afternoon. I have seen this kind of attitude turn into creative solutions through innovation and even a reinvention of an individual or an enterprise.

People frequently ask me what they are supposed to do when adversity is out of their direct control. Almost by definition, that is what makes a situation adverse, whether it's a cancer diagnosis or a global pandemic. My response is not to blame bad luck or angry gods but to face your challenges and embrace them. Cultivating this perspective can help you view adversity as a gift, and your ability to manage through tough times becomes your superpower. I am not suggesting, of course, that a cancer diagnosis is a gift. What I am saying is that regardless of what we confront, how we manage our troubles speaks to who we will become after they are gone from our lives. Most of the tactics for over-coming adversity are simply common sense. You should never be afraid to find the right kind of help, maintain your composure and humility, keep a positive attitude, and remember the big-picture goals.

My thoughts on adversity did not arise out of nowhere. There is an endless list of people whose greatness and accomplishments are marked by difficulties and failure. In fact, I think it's more of a common fac-tor for successful people and organizations than almost any other experience. The names of the companies and people who overcame great adversity might surprise you. Oprah Winfrey is known around the world as a wildly successful entrepreneur and entertainer, but the odds against her achievements were dramatically intimidating. Abused repeatedly by a cousin, uncle, and a family friend, she gave birth to a baby boy at age fourteen. She had to run away from home to escape mistreatment, and her child died after a short time. Winfrey, neverthe-less, finished high school, won awards for her oratory skills, and earned a full scholarship to college. Her talk show and film production com-pany became a media empire valued at more than $2 billion in 2022.

There are also people whose names you've likely never heard but whose products or businesses you have. When the dot-com bubble of the late '90s was creating an overabundance of new internet companies and absurd valuations, Nick Woodman started an online business to sell affordable electronics to a young demographic. Major retailers were able to beat his prices, and he never acquired the sales to become profitable. Undaunted, Woodman went back out to investors and pulled together almost $4 million for an online platform that awarded cash prizes for participating in various sweepstakes. FunBug, marketing through games, sounded like a good idea at that moment and showed growth early on, but the user base was not sustainable and the company folded.

Woodman, a surfer, took a break and went back to living out of his 1971 Volkswagen bus while trying to make a living selling 35mm cameras. An idea occurred to him—a way for athletes to carry video cameras while competing—so he attempted to attach a small camera to a Velcro strap worn on a surfer's wrist. The concept was tested out on a surfing trip to Australia, which made Woodman realize he needed to design and manufacture the cameras and not use off-the-shelf technology. Over the next decade, he refined his product and began growing a market of faithful users who attached the GoPro video cameras to motorcycles, bikes, race cars, airplanes, ski helmets, and their own bodies during competition or recreational sports. GoPros are also used widely in the film and video production industries. The reliability of the cameras and the quality of the video turned GoPro into a huge company and Nick Woodman into one of the world's youngest billionaires.

You have probably not heard of a company named Traf-O-Data and its device labeled the 8008, which was designed to read traffic tapes and process the data. The company's mission was to "read the raw data from roadway traffic counters and create reports for traffic engineers." The purpose was to control congestion and optimize traffic flow, but when the two young entrepreneurs, Bill Gates and Paul Allen, made their first sales pitch to a county, their machine failed during the demonstration. Failing is learning, though, for determined dreamers, and Allen later told friends that the Traf-O-Data bungle was seminal in leading the two partners to develop their first Microsoft product, which put them on a path to change business and much of the world.

Failure and adversity create a kind of feedback loop that teaches us what not to do, corrections to make in our designs and dreams, and the humility to keep our heads down and working. Use the information that comes from adversity and failure. There is almost always a piece of data that is useful and will inform your next steps. Successful people just keep grinding. I suspect, if we could ask him, James Dyson would offer the standard advice to never give up. You've probably seen

TV commercials for his bagless vacuum cleaners, which are now sold around the world. His persistence in the face of adversity makes his success even more legendary. While working on his concept of "cyclonic separation," Dyson made 5,127 failed prototypes for his vacuum. Fifteen years passed before he got his DC01 vacuum cleaner to the market in the year 1993.

Dyson's experience speaks to the Summit Mindset element of perspective during hard times. How did he view his thousands of failures? More than halfway through his list of attempts, Dyson's wife took on extra work, and he acknowledged they were dealing with "tough times" while also trying to raise three children. But each failure, he said, "brought me closer to solving the problem." This is an attitude famously expressed by Thomas Edison, who apparently failed almost twice as much as Dyson. Edison was struggling to invent the light bulb and it finally took him more than ten thousand tries to find a way to send electricity through a filament and get it to radiate light. When his friends criticized his constant failures over the years, the inventor said, "I have not failed. I've just found ten thousand ways that won't work."

So, how do we decide what is successful?

Wealth tends to be the measuring stick Americans use to determine success, but there are certainly other metrics. No writer, for instance, has ever found a wide audience without confronting insecurities and adversity. Robert M. Pirsig had an idea and determination. He wanted to discuss his favorite subject of philosophy and Western interpretations but was worried he would have few readers for such a book. His solution was to create a narrative of fictionalizing parts of a motorcycle ride across the northern plains with his young son and two close friends. Entitled *Zen and the Art of Motorcycle Maintenance*, Pirsig's discourse is about knowledge and philosophy, the concepts of good, history, science, Zen Buddhism, Greek philosophy, and the foundations of values. His purpose seems to have been to make the argument that nothing is more important than engagement with the world and the search for an understanding of quality. The imaginary conversations in his narrative tend to be with his former self, a character he named Phaedrus after

Socrates's dialogue in his writings. The real humans joining Pirsig on his seventeen-day trip were his son Chris and their family friends John and Sylvia Sutherland.

The aspiration that such a book might sell probably seemed absurd even to its author. Pirsig was using his adventure to examine notions like the romantic and classical views of the world. The romantic chooses to exist in the moment and take what is offered simply by being present while the classicist prefers to understand details, mechanics, inner workings, and what makes things as they are, which, Pirsig insisted to Phaedrus, made appreciation greater for all existence by engagement. His scrutiny was also turned toward projects like businesses and various efforts that faltered because of what he named a *gumption trap*. The definition he arrived at was a mindset or event that can "cause a person to lose enthusiasm and become discouraged from starting or continuing a project." Pirsig defined *gumption* as a combination of common sense, shrewdness, and a sense of initiative. How many start-up entrepreneurs and big achievers have gumption, and what percentage fall victim to the trap?[5]

Users of my Summit Mindset familiar with Pirsig's writing might identify similar lines of thought. In *Zen*, however, the philosopher spends a great deal of time, as have generations of thinkers, trying to identify what is generally referred to as *the good*, and whether it can even be defined. An entrepreneur might suggest the answer is yes, but often success in the age of technology and microchips comes with the arrival of *good enough*. The Summit Mindset, by contrast, is not a philosophical approach to life but is instead a practical application for living and succeeding. It is about perspective and effort. I have been drawn, however, to Pirsig's identification of dynamics that prevent achievement. He cites boredom, impatience, anxiety, and even excessive egotism, along with the possibility that an innovator or a project creator might not have the information necessary to succeed and that one aspect of a problem that needed solving might be more important than another that is getting disproportionate attention.

---

5   Robert M. Pirsig, *Zen and the Art of Motorcycle Maintenance* (Boston: Mariner Books, 1974).

Pirsig wrote about what he also described as *value and truth traps* as challenges that confront accomplishment. He questioned the use of a yes-no duality when trying to understand why an approach works and recommended reconsidering the context of questions or asking different ones that are more relevant. Advice he offered, which I think dramatically enhances the idea of my Summit Mindset, is to overcome our reluctance or inability to reevaluate our ideas because we are committed to a previous set of values. We need to, according to Pirsig, be ready to rediscover facts as they arise, recognize them when they are apparent and available, reassess the weight that is given current knowledge, and consciously decide to slow down to allow ourselves to process unstructured information.

It's important to mention Pirsig and his work for several reasons. His rationale both complements and supplements the Summit Mindset and is useful for anyone interested in my approach to life and business. In fact, he lists various factors that someone reaching the summit might want to always keep in mind. Egotism, which he elaborates on, can lead to belief in corrupted information or doubt of an inconvenient fact. He recommends for protection, as does the Summit Mindset, humility, modesty, attentiveness, and skepticism. Boredom is also described as a cause of sloppy work and must be addressed by stopping a project to rebuild common practices. Impatience, he insists, has the same destructive potential, and uncontrolled or measured anxiety might be the biggest obstacle to any success of a project. Pirsig said anxiety destroys confidence to even begin a task or seek a goal and work through it systematically. The solution he sees to overcome this disadvantage, which many of us face, is preparation and study, identifying the necessary detailed steps required, and trying to understand the "personhood and fallibility of professionals."

I mention Pirsig because, like me and others, he offers techniques to reach your summit and remain there, but I hold the writer and philosopher out as a superb example of persistence and my constant instruction to do the reps. As a thinker, Pirsig has great confidence in the clarity he brings to Western philosophy and believes his notion of a motorcycle trip and the fictitious version of his former self are a perfect vehicle to convey his thinking to a wider audience.

His task, though, was not completed with the writing of his final sentence. The book had to impress an agent and then be sold to a publisher before marketing to the public. This proved to require an even more monumental effort than his deft writing. Pirsig's manuscript was rejected 121 times before finding a publishing home. *Zen and the Art of Motorcycle Maintenance* sold five million copies worldwide in a matter of months, remained on best-seller lists for decades, and is still the most read book on philosophy ever published.

If 121 rejections is not adversity, then there is no such thing. What went through Pirsig's mind during that long period when he was being told no thank you? Surely his belief in himself and his writing, and the thinking that comprised his book's interior dialogue and analyses, must have wavered, at least slightly. Writers face these doubts. But Pirsig knew what he knew and was not going to relent, because he was confident in his book's story and its profoundly important themes about the human condition and the way we see the world. The 121 rejection letters gave him feedback to make edits and adjustments to his manuscript until it found a publisher. Robert M. Pirsig, in my interpretation, envisioned his summit, rode his motorcycle to the top, and never left. His journey became an American legend.

There are so many examples of how adversity was turned into accomplishment that it can appear like success is impossible without first being fed by adversity. Fire can bend iron, but it tempers steel and makes it stronger, and it can have the same effect on people who stand strong in their vision and determination. This is one of the foundational beliefs of the Summit Mindset, and it has made my life greater than I even dreamed.

Let adversity build you, not break you.

Exercises:

- **Prepare:** Certain types of adversity occur in almost everyone's life. The odds are you will likely lose a job at some point. Would you be ready to adjust if that happened? Do yourself a favor and plot out steps you would take to remedy your situation and find a new job. The first part would be how to respond and to whom? Who needs to know of the change of your status? Also, take the time now to look at your network. Are your professional relationships strong? Will certain people be more reliable than others? Make a short list of your strongest advocates to contact. Next, consider other lines of work where you might be happier or achieve greater things. What strengths would you bring to a new category of employment? Even more important, do an inventory of resources. How long can you survive without work? Will your savings give you enough time to make smart choices instead of hurried and worried ones?

- **Plan:** A financial or work crisis might appear considerably more likely than a natural disaster, but both can be mitigated with preparation. Make a plan to deal with natural disaster. Climate change is increasing the odds that we may all be exposed to dramatic events out of our control. If you live on a coast, in Tornado Alley, or in the earthquake zones of the West Coast, consider steps necessary after an event. What do you need in your house to survive a hurricane? How long can you go without electricity? Is your home likely to flood? Do you have a generator and gas? The same sort of protocol works to prepare for earthquakes, which can disrupt far worse than a hurricane. In Tornado Alley, do you have a safe place to go when a tornado warning is issued? Is your home insured against such a storm? These are just some of the questions you ought to answer to prepare for the adversity caused by a natural disaster.

CHAPTER SIX

CARING FOR OTHERS

Three things in human life are important: the first is to be kind; the second is to be kind; and the third is to be kind.

—HENRY JAMES

The critics of social media often complain about how the online platforms have prompted, and even amplified, the worst possible forms of behavior. I don't disagree that it has empowered bullies and facilitated anger, and, in some cases, even hatred. I also know that social media has promoted acts of kindness and positive outcomes for people in harmful situations, economic duress, or worse. You can find these stories easily on money-raising charitable platforms like GoFundMe, which allow caring people to come together and generate resources for those in need. Those efforts often are amplified on Facebook, Twitter, Instagram, and similar platforms. One friend can post a campaign to raise dollars for a family, individual, institution, or whatever they decide needs outside financial assistance, and in a matter of hours, there can be cash to resolve a crisis or help deal with personal loss.

Social media platforms Facebook, Twitter, LinkedIn, Instagram, and others can be used to amplify acts of kindness. I read of a young man in Nebraska who ordered his dinner from one of the delivery services, and when the driver arrived in a beat-up and rattling automobile, he had a conversation with her as he paid his bill. The exchange led to this gentleman, whose name was Jonathan, asking about her daily struggles. The driver said she didn't even have the $450 to pay her monthly rent, and he offered to go to an ATM and get her the money. When he returned, Jonathan got contact info for her landlord and agreed to Venmo him the driver's next four months of rent. The act of caring seemed purely altruistic.

Jonathan posted about his gift on his Twitter account, hoping to inspire his followers to help others, when possible, but was, in more than a few responses, accused of "virtue signaling." This is when people believe you are posting about your generous acts to make yourself look good and not necessarily simply to be kind and helpful. Regardless of whether his motivation was self-aggrandizement, Jonathan's kindness appeared to have motivated others on his timeline to do the same thing, and their numbers overwhelmed the people who were accusing him of tending to his ego. I choose to believe Jonathan helped the delivery lady because he had the resources and was inspired to do something kind, knowing that his generosity would do as much for his spirit as it did for her comfort and security, and might even prompt similar acts of generosity.

In my previous discussions about the Summit Mindset and establishing the four pillars that guide our lives, I mentioned that *others* were central to my happiness and well-being and were one of my pillars. I wasn't simply referring to my family and friends. My belief has long been that our lives are better when we think about other people, including strangers, and how we might help. I think everyone should make other people one of their four pillars. I believe we are made greater by our willingness to perform even small acts of kindness to improve the situations of strangers and acquaintances. An opened door, an encouraging word, a compliment—these are all gestures that can make the difference in another person's day, and, on occasion, their life.

People often see offering help as a daunting task and are overwhelmed trying to find meaningful ways to assist, but it is not necessary to search for big things to offer. My days of living with a Summit Mindset have been constructed around actions, not just intentions. I try to make serving others, personally and professionally, a part of my daily living. Your simple actions and gestures can become the most meaningful event in someone else's day, and even their life. Everyone can find what works best for them, but I have found that even a short conversation with a stranger at the grocery store gets a positive reaction. My goal is always to plant a seed that might inspire. I have frequently left notes with generous tips at my local restaurants that say, "Thanks for the great service. #DreamAwake," and I've had young servers stop me on the street where I live and tell me they framed my note and keep it near their bed as inspiration and motivation.

I have, in fact, developed a daily ritual that keeps me focused on others and grateful for my life. Morning begins with silence and prayer and a communication of gratitude for simply being alive and having the gift of pursuing happiness for another day. My next step is to send out twenty-five personal texts to people to whom I am the closest, but many times this might include a new person who has touched my life. This is not a group text. Everyone gets a personal note, no matter where I am in the world or what time zone, to ask how they are doing or to offer encouragement on what they're doing in their lives. I send these texts seven days a week, all year long, to let people close to me know that I care and am thinking about them.

Why am I telling you this? To demonstrate that our singular efforts can make a difference, and often have a ripple effect. Another example occurred when my wife and I were leaving a favorite spot after breakfast. One of the waitresses stopped us on the way out and asked if I would have coffee with her boyfriend, Chase, a young man whose energy and work diligence I had noticed and admired. She said he had recently gotten out of jail after making a foolish mistake and had no friends since he was new in town. I said that I'd be happy to get together with Chase, and we began a text conversation. We both liked to run and began our friendship with conversations during our workouts. He opened up about his background, sharing with me his hopes, fears, and dreams for his life. I encouraged him to take night classes in college and start a secondary education, which he did, eventually receiving his diploma. Chase and I shared many stories during those morning runs and became close friends. He is on my morning list of twenty-five people I contact daily for encouragement and inspiration—not only for him but for me too.

Each of us can have a similar impact on the lives of others if we make caring a part of our daily actions. There are people, though, who feel called to make a profound difference, and we can use their examples to inspire our efforts. I learned about a couple in the Texas Hill Country who made it their life's work to help children who had been harmed by their parents or while in foster care. Their work began with a modest dream of creating a safe environment for a few children in a small rural community and has turned into a forty-five-year legacy of caring that will live for generations.

Gary Priour grew up on a large ranch outside Kerrville, Texas, near the town of Ingram. He went away to Harvard and earned a degree in 1969, majoring in English literature. When he fell in love, he moved to Oregon with his wife and they had a son, but when the marriage failed, Gary became a single father. He was operating a day care center when a mother dropped off her three-year-old daughter and never returned. Gary was left with two children, his son, and the neighbor's little girl. Returning to Texas had given him an idea, though. He asked his father for three hundred acres of land to build a youth ranch for abused and abandoned children. Initially, Gary said his father thought the notion was ridiculous, but he agreed.

There was no money to build dorms for the kids, but volunteers began to show up with resources. Donations came at just the right time. A telethon was held on local TV. Grants were sought and won. Community leaders gave endorsements. Needs were always met, and the Hill Country Youth Ranch began to take shape. Eventually, the state of Texas sent him its most in-need children from government custody. Often, Child

Protective Services was unable to manage children who had been sexually abused, abandoned, or physically mistreated while in foster homes.

Gary, whose stature suggests the size of his great heart, had fallen in love again and married Carol, and they worked together to expand the ranch. Money was donated for an arts center and then an equestrian ring, and horses were provided. Year after year, the ranch grew and the love and caring spread. The ranch kids attended local public schools and participated on athletic teams and in extracurricular activities sanctioned by the local school district. They excelled when they were supposed to be cast aside. Gary and Carol managed to pull together funding to increase housing, and the ranch capacity grew. But there was still great need.

In a beautiful valley not far from the youth ranch, a woman named Oma Bell Perry had heard of Gary and Carol's great work. As a young woman, she had inherited a ranch at the headwaters of the Frio River and called it the "Land of 11,000 Springs." Perry's family legacy went back to the founding of Texas; she was a descendant of Stephen F. Austin, the man who had arranged for land grants from Mexico for US settlers. Perry decided the best use for her family's vast holdings was to deed them over to the Hill Country Youth Ranch, and money began to arrive to build dormitories and a school. Children who had suffered in bad situations were now playing in the cool waters of a river outside their door and learning from people who loved and cared about them. The box canyon eventually became known in nearby towns as the "Valley of Angels."

There was even more magic to follow, though. Ed and Trudy Bruni, who were touring the Hill Country, stopped at a thrift store managed by the ranch. While shopping, they asked about the ranch and if it was having success helping children. They asked for a tour, and Gary showed them around with his usual sense of purpose and humility. The Brunis asked what else might be needed in the valley, and Gary had said he hoped to raise the money to build a charter school and a library, though the cost might reach several million dollars. Ed was a retired longshoreman from the Houston Ship Channel and had coached high school football while Trudy had raised their children. Their economic profile did not suggest they could become significant donors. Gary was certainly not expecting a donation, and was shocked when they offered to pay for the school and library. How? Ed had invested $10,000 in his nephew's start-up company, which became wildly successful and made him a millionaire many times over. Trudy and Ed were happy to be able to share their wealth with young people whose lives were being rebuilt one day, one book, and one caring adult at a time.

During the forty-five-year existence of the Hill Country Youth Ranch, an estimated four thousand children have been raised and educated, with many becoming teachers, truckers, scientists, homemakers, cooks, and entrepreneurs. They have contributed greatly to their communities with their work and their taxes. The love and caring they now bring to their families and friends make them unlikely to repeat the patterns of abuse they experienced because that cycle has been broken by received love.

Gary and Carol have now turned over management of the ranch to one of its former residents, though they offer advice and continuing guidance, and everyone in Kerrville expects the important work of the Hill Country Youth Ranch to continue for many more generations. Gary, a man of abiding faith in his God, believes his work and the serendipitous good fortune of money and assistance was more about providence than his personal efforts.

"We've always stayed committed to our mission, and God did the rest," he said. "I remain amazed at what God has done. It looks to me like, if we follow the trail of guidance the Father leaves in the clues of daily life, we, and the children we care for, are heirs to a legacy of miracles."

Gary and Carol Priour are an example of the power of an idea and what can be accomplished with determination and a commitment to a vision of caring for others. Throughout the course of their more than four decades of building and operating the Hill Country Youth Ranch, they never faltered in striving to improve the lives of innocent young people harmed by adults who were supposed to provide them love and support for their healthy growth. Of course, we can't all make our entire lives about public service and doing good, but if one person can come up with such a powerful concept like Gary Priour did, changing the lives of so many, then we should never underestimate our own ability to help others and keep them in our consciousness as part of our daily endeavors.

Business involvement is essential to the task and responsibility of helping people, too. In an earlier chapter, I discussed Corporate Social Responsibility and the engagement of businesses in their communities and even the wider world. While the label for the practice might be relatively new, the concept has been around for about seventy years. Public awareness of the behavior of businesses increased with the advent of the internet and handheld wireless devices. For good or ill, the acts of businesses large and small can be public knowledge quickly, influencing brand image and profits and loss. The combined moral and financial power of businesses can profoundly impact the lives of millions of people, which has created the societal pressures for large corporations and small companies to do more than just pursue profits and shareholder values.

CSR encompasses more than just philanthropic efforts by a business. Archie Carroll, who developed the Pyramid of Corporate Social Responsibility, described the obligations of being a good corporate citizen with his 1991 introduction of the concept.[6] The four corners of the pyramid include factors like the legal responsibility of obeying relevant local and international laws; being ethical and avoiding causing harm by remaining just, moral, and fair; engaging in community investment as your profit grows; and giving back to society to improve your relevant communities. These legal, philanthropic, ethical, and economic responsibilities will sustain vibrant businesses and the customers and communities they serve. Giving back in the twenty-first century also includes being aware of environmental risks and climate change. In the most basic sense, caring for others also means protecting the

---

6   Denise Baden, "A Reconstruction of Carroll's Pyramid of Corporate Social Responsibility for the 21st Century," *International Journal of Corporate Social Responsibility* 1, no. 8 (August 2, 2016), https://jcsr. springeropen.com/articles/10.1186/s40991-016-0008-2.

environment in which we all live, and businesses are expected to do everything reasonably possible to reduce any harmful effects their products and services might have on the ecosystem of our planet.

Nonetheless, when the energy and ideas of individuals are combined with corporate resources, a greater good can be realized. I took advantage of that notion when I became the CEO of global juice drink company Tampico. Our leadership team discussed creating a culture focused on a spirit of giving back, designed to serve all our relevant communities while making a difference for our employees. The energy and innovation for much of our effort came from the inspired work and leadership of our employee Erika Lopez, who was my executive assistant. Marshaling the talents of people on your staff is central to creating programs that succeed inside and outside the walls of a business. Galvanizing groups of people to work as one is, to me, the magic that a smart business can offer to create social value beyond its products. Erika established practices and worked with employees and leadership to launch our giving platforms, and we began to raise money for various charitable organizations. While our company was relatively unknown compared to other better advertised brands, our employees came together to raise substantial amounts of cash and other resources to groups like Casa Central, Ronald McDonald House, Reading in Motion, Give Kids the World Village, Chicago Scholars, and Feeding America. We were proud to be a part of charitably contributing to our communities, but something even greater happens when a company's employees are standing next to each other packing bags of groceries at the local food bank or painting the interior of schools in underprivileged neighborhoods of Chicago. The establishment of our Tampico foundation formalized our culture of giving back through community involvement, which quickly became a part of our brand's DNA. Employees were empowered with paid time off to take part in their favorite charities and fund-raise on a scheduled basis.

A recent refinement of the concept of CSR is described as *skills-based volunteerism* (SBV). The idea behind SBV is to channel specific skills of a company's employees to be used by nonprofit organizations.

A report from the *Stanford Social Innovation Review* indicates that more than 50 percent of companies are focusing charitable efforts on sending people with the right skills to the right organizations to improve the efforts of the nonprofit. Corporate expertise on strategic planning, technology, finance, marketing, and operations can now be offered to a nonprofit that might not otherwise get such professional knowledge. SBV has been shown to improve employee engagement and retention. When they return to the office after helping a nonprofit, their work quality is often improved.[7]

The Stanford study suggests that traditional philanthropic efforts by companies tend to be transactional with grants and volunteer days, and that approach generally has little lasting effect. According to the report, "What makes skills-based volunteering different and important is that when it works, it knits together the expertise and resources from corporate and nonprofit sectors to create strengthened sustainable solutions that don't come undone when partners go their separate ways." It should also be obvious that people in the nonprofit sector will develop their skills while working with corporate volunteers on a long-term basis, and the businesses providing the skilled volunteers are likely to develop a talent pool of individuals in the organization they are aiding. Something much greater happens, in my view, when both parties are working together toward a common good over a longer period. Learning, growth, and friendships develop. I see this attitude spreading to the wider community in almost every case and positively affecting other efforts to help, if only by inspiration.

I long ago became convinced of the inherent goodness in people, and I think Corporate Social Responsibility is a broader manifestation of that. Some companies have gone beyond the values of CSR and have dedicated their business models to assisting people and organizations. These are entrepreneurs driven more by helping than making a profit. I had never

7   Christine Letts and Danielle Holly, "The Promise of Skills Based Volunteering," *Stanford Social Innovation Review* 15, no. 4 (Fall 2017): 41–47, https://ssir.org/articles/entry/the_promise_of_skills_based_volunteering.

heard of traditional businesses devoting 100 percent of their profits to a cause and was amazed when I learned of the mission of Bulwark Coffee Company. Founded by former Marine Rich Turner, Bulwark's purpose is described as "serving those who serve." Turner was a Marine Corps attack helicopter pilot, forward air controller, and military liaison. Upon leaving the service, he began a promising career in corporate business but found it was not fulfilling.

"When I left the Marine Corps and dove into my next career in corporate America," he said, "I felt an emptiness in it. I missed serving a greater purpose, a cause greater than my own career ambitions. Perhaps, that is why many of my fellow Marines found themselves serving as firefighters, police officers, or emergency medical personnel."

Turner decided people on the front line of public service needed help and recognition, and he did not want to rely on government support. He focused his efforts on assisting police officers, first responders, firefighters, and veterans. He would commit all his company's profits to the unique needs of those who serve, everything from "tactical rescue operations in contested environments, aid delivery, mental health resources, equipment, equine therapy, scholarships." Turner pledged to provide any resource to facilitate bettering their lives "by supporting their unmet needs and recognizing their unique commitment to serve their country and community."

Next to petroleum, coffee is the second most traded commodity in the world and the second most consumed beverage after water. Turner has designed his company to serve three purposes using the commodity of coffee. He points out that 70 percent of firefighters in the US are volunteers and that 70 percent of fire departments are donor funded. Much of their time and energy is spent raising funds to repair or replace aging equipment. Bulwark commits financial support to firefighters, as well as police officers and veterans by assisting with needed resources as they readjust their lives back to civilian environments.

"BCC [Bulwark Coffee Company] is taking a leading role in showing its support to first responders by donating 100% of its profits to support these brave men and women," Turner explains on his website.

"BCC intends to reintroduce communities to the selfless service of the heroes that walk among them. With every purchase of our coffee products, community members will be able to directly contribute to the heroes of their local community." Bulwark's direct-to-consumer retail model is offering premium coffees from various producers, which are, according to Turner, only the beginning of a range of products "to eventually support every facet of the lives of our heroes through sustainable community involvement, because wars, disasters, and emergencies are only becoming more frequent. Besides, it is the least we can do to support these men and women in uniform."

Not all of us can live our lives with the singularity of purpose exhibited by Rich Turner, but we can use intentional dedication to help others and make a difference. I also believe we can accomplish much by making a conscious decision to be servants. By choosing "others" as one of your four pillars in the Summit Mindset, you take action to be aware of the needs of people outside your circle of family and friends. By deciding to be a helper, as a donor or volunteer or other method you might find to assist someone, you actualize your intentions and become a servant, which, I think, is the greatest accomplishment any person might strive for.

I believe it is important to recognize we are all equal, regardless of our circumstances. The homeless man with his hand out is every bit as important as you or me. When you believe this, you learn to listen and truly hear how you might help. If our goal is to aid, then we must hear what is being said. When you hear the details of their story, you can better understand how to help. Otherwise, we are indulging in an act of vanity, in my view, because our only outcome is to make ourselves feel good for offering something, even if it might not be anything that can help the person. What if they only need a few dollars for a bus ticket home but you have judged they are addicted to drugs and must get into treatment? Caring requires understanding how to best assist others; we must listen closely.

To truly help, there also must be a willingness to allow the experience to unfold and let it take you beyond the initial encounter. There is always the possibility of a transformative moment for the helper as much as there is for the person who has been helped. Stories feed our spiritual needs, and I believe there is great service and healing in letting people share their experiences with you. Be open to acquaintances, too, who you know only casually but who need you in a way you are unaware of. Look for insights during conversations, be ready to help or ask questions that get a person to tell you what they are dealing with, and be ready to help. It is not uncommon for the helper to end up being the one who gets helped.

I had this personal experience with a friend I met through my son's involvement in wrestling. After a few meets, I got to know Vinnie, whose boy was on the team with mine. We talked frequently about our sons, and as the conversations broadened, we spoke of our work and health and our lives in the town where we lived. Vinnie shared with me one evening that he'd had a bout with stomach cancer but that he was in remission. We remained only acquaintances through the years, but one evening at a wrestling match after our boys had reached high school, Vinnie told me that his cancer had aggressively returned. I offered sympathy and asked how else I might be able to help.

Vinnie's son Jack had reached the age of confirmation in his church, and I was a bit surprised when he asked me to be his sponsor. I was honored but wondered if, perhaps, there was a family member who ought to stand with his son for the ceremony. Vinnie made it clear, however, he wanted me in Jack's life, and I was honored by his asking. I understood his request and its emotional context and had no further questions.

Vinnie's health, unfortunately, continued to deteriorate. We began to speak more, and I tried to provide comfort for him to converse openly and to be vulnerable. I shared with him my health struggles and my fears at that time that I might not recover. The two of us were emotional enough to cry, and when he was hospitalized, Vinnie's wife asked me to spend time with him, which was what I had wanted since we had, predictably, become close friends. He had come to understand that his time was growing short, and his family gathered around him at the hospital every day. His wife and children were constantly present, and his extended family assembled each morning near his bed.

When they left, I showed up. Vinnie needed me to talk to, and we spent the nights of his final time in emotional conversations about our lives, praying and crying together as friends and brothers. My friend was a hardworking, decent, and honorable man who possessed great physical strength and a love for his family, and it was difficult to watch him be diminished by disease. On his final day, the hospital room was filled with family and friends, but Vinnie and I found time to pray. He was strong and peaceful as he took his last breaths. His life might have been shortened, but he had lived it well, and I was grateful to have made his friendship.

The other gift I was given by Vinnie was the friendship with his son. Jack is a part of my daily life and is on my text list of twenty-five people I reach out to every morning. Vinnie's son is leading a productive and purposeful life, and I've been privileged to be a part of it. My experience of becoming a friend with his father has also led me to believe we were brought together for a reason. I have always looked to plant seeds with people and hope for something to grow that would be of service to others, and that motivation never leaves me. Gandhi said giving is a selfish act because it makes us feel better, and it does, but that is a net positive effect. I believe it is an essential part of living a fulfilled and meaningful life and that we are all better people when we make others central to our time, if only part of the time.

You can assist people in so many ways that even a partial list can become exhaustive. We can all be creative, though, and come up with ideas to help. If, for example, you receive gifts that you don't need, consider redirecting them to a charity. The giver of that gift might be touched by your act and inspired to make a similar donation. If you see someone unhoused on the street, asking for money, you might consider offering to buy them food. Money is not always the best idea because it can be used for drugs or alcohol, but providing something to eat to a person living on the street is almost always appreciated and leaves a positive impact on the struggling individual. You might even consider sharing the meal with the stranger and hearing their story. People do not choose to be unhoused.

I also like the idea of helping people get active in their lives. We all know someone who is low energy and has stopped exercising. Because we live in a sedentary culture that invites us to sit and stare at screens all day, encouraging someone to become active can have profound effects. It might require a bit of diplomacy, but you could consider starting with just an offer to take a walk and have a conversation.

Offering to do a chore for someone is also a sign of caring and could come at precisely the right time a person is overwhelmed with tasks and responsibilities. Mowing someone's lawn, washing their car, running an errand, or picking up around their place has the potential to grow a friendship and change the outcome of someone's day and even their perspective on life.

We can alter our perspectives by helping others. Various scientific studies have suggested that people who do good deeds become changed by these acts, even if they have consistently displayed characteristics of being manipulative, narcissistic, and psychopathic. Southern Methodist University professor Nathan Hudson describes those traits as the "Dark Triad" and says they can be realistically reduced by making yourself perform acts of kindness for others. His study supports the idea that "donating money to charity that you would normally spend on yourself" or "talking to a stranger and asking them about themselves" results in decreasing the Dark Triad traits within just four months. Hudson did a survey of more than 420 students over the age of twenty and discovered that those who decided to improve their personalities by exhibiting kindness and thoughtful behaviors were able to show more extraversion, agreeableness, openness, conscientiousness, and emotional stability. These transformations can have broad social implications, too, because people who display Dark Triad traits are shown by earlier studies to have negative behaviors like criminal activity, intimate partner violence, cheating in school, and bad behavior at work.

What my Summit Mindset urges is that we make doing for others central to our personalities and the rhythm of our days. We can create a kind of reliable pathology for our own behavior and, cumulatively, we make a difference over time. None of us is likely to have great impact on the world, but we can affect people and might even alter the course of their lives with a helping hand or the kind of outreach that lets them know there are others who care. As the Dalai Lama has said, "If you want others to be happy, practice compassion. If you want to be happy, practice compassion."

Exercises:

- **Challenge:** Encourage yourself to begin helping others as part of your daily activities. You don't have to do something for someone every day, but be mindful and see what opportunities pop up where you could lend a hand. Make a list of people you know who might need a kindness or some assistance with where they are in their lives. Make a separate category of the types of help you might be able to provide, whether that is teaching them something simple like how to send an email or offering your skills as an auto mechanic to make costly vehicle repairs more affordable and less onerous for their budget. We all have valuable talents, and they become even more useful when we engage them to help others.

- **Create a Tool Kit:** Think of simple things you can do regularly that might make a difference, and keep them in mind during the routines of daily life. These might be as basic as teaching someone a skill that you use regularly in your life or work. Be willing to listen when you sense someone needs to talk. Offer counsel when appropriate. Become a person who helps others get things done, whether that is finally painting a fence or getting legal documents filed and completed for a friend. Helping can become a habit when you create a tool kit of your best abilities to deploy in the service of others. Your "helper's tool kit" is nothing more than a list of characteristics you have to offer another person or a skill they might need use of, which you have already acquired.

CHAPTER SEVEN

FOLLOWING FAITH

Faith is the bird that feels the light when the dawn is still dark.

—**RABINDRANATH TAGORE**

Writing, even talking, about faith is tricky and complicated, but the spiritual is an essential part of my life, and I want to communicate its importance because I know there are many others who struggle with it. Many of you reading this who adopt the Summit Mindset are likely to make faith one of your Four Pillars. Obviously, faith and my deep and abiding belief in God comprises one of the four corners of the foundation that guides me, and I think it is important to address. I am not a theologian, cosmologist, religion scholar, or member of the clergy. I am, however, a person who has always felt it important to have a spiritual life, and I do. It has provided me hope and strength when passing through the difficult phases that we all confront from time to time, and because it is so central to the lives of so many others, I wanted to offer my thinking around faith and how it works with my Summit Mindset.

Spirituality is easier to feel than it is to define. A fundamental belief of probably most of the planet's population is there is something greater than our little speck of dust floating through the incomprehensible vastness of space. There might just be an instinct among humans that because we are sentient, we want to feel a connection to something greater than us, a power beyond our understanding but an important dynamic of being alive. For me, this is my belief in God. We don't know if such a thing exists because it is, quite simply, unknowable. Science has never provided a proof of the existence of God, or what philosopher Aristotle once described as the "Prime Mover," and that might never happen, but we humans keep asking, what is the purpose of our time in this world? We want to know meaning, to connect all the pieces of existence into one rational and scientific explanation. I doubt there is a person living, or who has ever lived, who has looked up at a clear night sky filled with stars and hasn't felt a yearning to know and understand the entire fabric of the universe, who we are, and what we are doing here. Maybe the ache and emptiness many of us sometimes feel is a distance from a creator or the source of all that has caused the universe to come into being, whatever that might be. Perhaps we are already connected but simply haven't paid attention or become aware because we have not practiced faith or even basic mindfulness.

I realize this is a bit of an existential topic for a book of this nature and that what is important to me may be of no consequence to you. However, people trying to live a more purposeful life and pursue happiness often find themselves contemplating what it means to be spiritual. I don't think it requires joining a church or choosing a religion to practice, though those are practicable ways of exploring your spirituality. What becomes important for me is an underlying sense that I am connected to something greater than myself, which is my God, and I take both comfort and strength from what my heart tells me is true and right. I don't know what that something might be, what exactly is God, but I have unwavering faith in a deity's existence. I also know that if I can do good, live a meaningful life and help others, be charitable and hopeful through struggles, I might make some tiny contribution to whatever is greater than us and is the life force of our existence, and that provides me another sense of fulfillment. Is that God? I don't know, but I believe it is and have always known that in my heart and soul. Faith helps me bridge the distance between what science doesn't know about the existence of God and what my heart knows with great certainty. I don't, however, try to place boundaries on my faith; I just know it is important and has value.

Spirituality and faith do not need to be overly mysterious and profound, though. Even members of the clergy want to make it more accessible by simplifying what for them may have been a complex emotional and intellectual journey to become involved in practicing their religion as a leader of others. Faith, for me, is a deeply held conviction, intellectual and emotional, that there is something going on that is greater than me. I know that to be the presence of God in my life, and I accept that there are profoundly held beliefs in the idea that the universe exists as a god. I don't know what other people feel, but I know without a doubt that the spiritual is a part of me through God, and I am connected to that mystery. In a practical sense, though, I think I found the simplest and most enduring definition of faith years ago when I heard a member of the clergy ask a couple of profound questions of his congregants. Trying to find language that defines faith can be difficult, but the questions from a Catholic priest that I heard helped me find practical understanding of spirituality, which gives it more relevance in our contemporary existence. Taking the measure of our lives as we reach the end, he suggested there were two questions that would help everyone determine if they had lived spiritually.

"Did you love more than you hated?" he asked. "Did you give more than you took?"

These are questions worth asking of ourselves daily, and a utilitarian approach to living a life of faith. This makes your belief system personal and not institutional, which is how I choose to live my life. I am not, of course, trying to imply that churches are without value and importance. I am simply suggesting that I have discovered what gives me comfort and confidence, and maybe help users of the Summit

Mindset find answers, not necessarily in the stars but rather in what is right in front of them. Those who are not religious live by this principle too. Anthropologists have estimated that humanity has identified more than three thousand different gods, goddesses, animals, and objects to worship, which means we can spend a great deal of time finding a belief system that appeals to our spiritual needs. In the end, giving more than you take and loving more than you hate is a method for living that anyone can access.

Maybe there is just a compulsion among humans to find meaning where, perhaps, none exists. My belief is that if we decide an event in our lives has importance and influence, we want that to have happened for a reason. I know many people who have no religion, who are secular humanists and atheists, who are convinced "everything happens for a reason." If you believe that, does it not follow that it becomes true? Doesn't that give us comfort and remove us from living in a world of random action and chaos? Remember my story about Vinnie? I knew from the time we began our friendship that he was placed in my path for a purpose because I was willing to help people. I was convinced my perspective, my distance from his family, gave me objectivity on his personal health crisis. What I didn't mention is that, even though I knew a few of Vinnie's longtime friends and family and they were complete strangers to me, Vinnie's wife understood the importance of my relationship with her late husband and asked me to do his eulogy. Throughout the memorial service people kept approaching me and asking, "Who are you? I never heard of you. It's like Vinnie wanted a stranger to do his eulogy."

This has happened many times in my life, and I don't think that's chance. I believe it was God. I will accept that perhaps we are simple beings trying to assign meaning to our lives. Are we important enough that our actions are directed? Maybe that's not it. I've often heard people say that when you are open to possibilities, the universe sends them in your direction. I think it's possible Vinnie crossed my path because I had a mindset that I wanted, I was willing to help others, and God brought us together. Even secular thinkers can be convinced that there is a sentient force at work in the universe that might be guiding positive evolution and daily outcomes. I only know what my faith tells me, and that is we are all traveling on roads that lead to the same place, though most of us don't exactly know where that might be. I believe we are all on a path back home to God.

Faith, of course, is not science, and as human intelligence advances, people want proof of ideas. There is a reluctance in our culture to believe in things we cannot see, know with certainty, or touch. I know there is something greater than me, and by being aware of that I give more meaning to my life. Meaningful lives certainly do not require an element of faith, but when I experienced traumatic difficulties, I have found that it was my faith and prayers that pulled me out of those dark spots. Even when I was lain low by bad health or personal challenges, the faith that I had begun to feel even more strongly through my years of practicing the Summit Mindset is what gave me the will and the hope I needed to survive. That same faith will tell you it is a virtual certainty you will encounter adversity but that you will have what you need to endure and grow through that experience. We get bruised and cut by living, but I have chosen to accept the scars—love them, in fact—and be a person of faith rather than living a life of fear.

It is certainly possible to live with a Summit Mindset and not rely on faith as one of your four pillars. There can be four other dynamic factors that you think will guide you and give you greater potential to become what you dream and find happiness. Humans, though, I think are inherently spiritual. We don't seem to want to believe that we are simply born, live, and die, and that is the end of it for us individually. The meaning we search for, however, tends to be, as I have suggested, unknowable, and our reaction is to rely on faith to bridge the gap between what is certain and what we feel is true. We know that something is true so strongly that it becomes a truth in our hearts and minds, or maybe we sense a connection to a force far greater than ourselves and it gives us the context in which to live. I have found that by struggling to reach the summit and knowing that I can do what is necessary to stay there even through the most difficult of adversities, that my faith in God is what gives me that confidence—faith that my will and the influence of something greater will empower me to stand into whatever winds are blowing.

My essential goal with the Summit Mindset, as I've explained throughout this book, is to give people some fundamental tools to help make their lives more fulfilling and happier. I am not interested in pushing religious or spiritual belief systems. However, I did want to reveal my thinking on how these topics affect my daily endeavors and how they are practically applied in the chance they might provide guidance to the reader. I make no judgments on anyone who has found the comfort and spiritual strength they need from their religious and moral beliefs, and, yes, their god. There are, though, uncountable numbers of secularists who believe kindness is their god and to do good is their religion, to paraphrase Thomas Paine. Even though humans have been searching for explanations of reality since we came out of caves and named gods who oversaw thunder and lightning and fire, maybe it's possible we have overcomplicated our search for understanding and that to know God and spirituality is nothing more than being kind and doing good.

Gods weren't just our primitive explanations for natural phenomena, though. Religions and gods through the millennia seem to have grown out of the human need to understand and attempt to explain death. This is why over the past few thousand years various religions have relied on resurrection stories and theology. The idea that life can be eternal can remove the fears of death, and we empower gods to give us this gift. But even as religions were evolving with this kind of intellectual and emotional structure, ancient philosophers were trying to create a way of living that provided meaning and comfort without the spiritual. Technically, these philosophical teachings and discussions, particularly by the Greeks, did not always go into the matter of God, but they also were not strictly making arguments for atheism. The great thinkers of that day were doing what we humans have been trying to accomplish from the time we became cognitive, and that is to find a kind of template for living a good and happy life, which is why their rationale is worth examining. As presumptuous as it might sound, I think I am trying to do the same thing for contemporaneous living with my Summit Mindset.

If you've had philosophy classes in high school or college, chances are good you came across a Greek thinker called Epicurus. His logic was designed to end the fear of death, which he thought led to better living, and his philosophy can be seen on tombstones all across the reaches of ancient Rome's empire: "I was not; I am; I am not; I do not care." Epicurus argued that the fear of death grew out of a belief that there was awareness of being dead. "Death," he insisted, "is nothing to us. When we exist, death is not and when death exists, we are not." Consciousness and pleasure, he believed, ended with death, which meant that in death there was neither pleasure nor pain.

Philosophers of the antiquity wanted to reject the idea of God or gods and said their stories of punishment in the afterlife were ridiculous superstitions. They were offering a logic to suggest a life without a god could be well lived and fulfilling, and what might be considered spiritual was not essential. Christianity and Islam were spreading across the cradles of civilization, though, and what came to be known as Epicurean logic faced great resistance. People wanted protection from death and believed in spirituality. Epicurus insisted to his followers that most human suffering was caused by the irrational fears of death and possible retribution in the afterlife for bad behaviors in this one. His arguments seemed to imply that if death is no cause for fear, why do humans need their gods? In a letter to an associate in Greece, Epicurus told him, "Accustom thyself to believe that death is nothing to us, seeing that, when we are, death is not come, and, when death is come, we are not." His ethics were also built around four key constructs: we ought not fear God, or worry about death, and he believed that what is good is easy to get and that which is terrible is easy to endure. Epicurus thought the best life was one lived wisely, soberly, and morally, and that humans could determine those standards even without the guidance of a god.

There are a thousand arguments to be made challenging Epicurean logic, and just as many on its behalf. I shared that brief bit of ancient history to suggest that there will always be different ways of living and viewing the world on matters of God and spirituality. As I suggest with the Summit Mindset, you don't have to be a member of a certain church or believe in a god to be a spiritual person. In fact, there are alternative beliefs and constructs that allow us to still seek some form of spirituality without adhering to traditionalized religions that dominate the planet. Pantheism, for instance, is a conviction that the entire concept of the universe as it presently exists is God. Pantheism holds that the combined substances, laws, and forces we see in our existing universe comprise the complete manifestation of God. A separate doctrine called panentheism allows for a God that includes all the universe but claims that is only part of the entire being. There are notions, too, like agnostic theism in which adherents believe in God but not religion, and they regard the basis of their convictions in God's existence to be inherently unknowable. Omnists, though, recognize and respect all religions and their various gods. They sometimes qualify their belief system by saying that all religions contain truths but that no single religion provides all the truth that exists regarding God.

When I expressed the unfaltering conviction that Vinnie was placed into my life for a reason, it implied that I thought there was a higher power at work, which, of course, I believe to be God. If that is the case, I have no idea what the purpose might be of our meeting, other than the support and friendship we provided each other, and, ultimately, his friends and family. My faith that our meeting has importance, however, continues. Maybe I was supposed to learn from going through his suffering with him, or I was sent there for no other cause than to help him deal with the end of his life. I realize, though, that people want there to be importance in their choices and a value that suggests that they are even guided in certain directions. This thinking gives quality and deeper purpose to our lives instead of believing an event like meeting with Vinnie is a random incident; it takes on an almost mysterious weight and context because that higher power wanted me there. I may not know why, but I have faith that we were brought together for a reason. I have never tried to define what that guiding power is for other people, whether it is God or even a force that transcends traditional ideas of God. I simply know through my faith that I am connected to something far greater than myself, which is why it is one of my four pillars of my life in the Summit Mindset.

My spirituality and faith are covered by the idea known as theological determinism, which is a belief that everything is predestined to happen by a god who dictates every moment in existence. I don't think I fit completely into this categorical description of faith because I am not certain that me running into someone on the street and having that turn into a friendship is a trifle that God might be bothered with, but I still want to believe that it was God or the universe steering me. I can still have faith that there was a purpose without thinking that the precise moment was predetermined by an omnipotent deity. The concept that the future is already fixed because God has divine foreknowledge of every miniscule moment of time and events can be hard to both grasp and accept because it removes the exercise of our free will, but I know what I know, and it gives me strength when I need it and hope when I am down.

Most of the people, I am confident, who will adopt the Summit Mindset are likely to be people of faith, either the religious or the secular variety. This conclusion is why I wanted to offer my thinking and, indeed, even my feelings around the subject, as well as some history. I think the more we understand the beginnings and impacts of the elements of our lives, the more we can use them to improve ourselves and increase our potential to help others, which are reasons faith is so central to me and why I made it one of my pillars. I realize that some people cannot believe in things they are unable to see, but faith lives in what is probably best described as a metaphysical realm, and not the physical. I see my faith in God as a force that goes beyond just hope and lives in my heart and spirit while also providing me a purpose. I think it would really be hard to find reason in living without my faith. People who live this way, spiritually and with faith, have a deep and unfailing belief that no matter how bad their situation, things are going to turn out just fine. I think there is a strong argument to be made that for most humans, faith is the foundation of their existence and provides nourish-ment for their heart and soul.

Faith makes the case for itself. Accepting faith as a fact and acknowl-edging its power, I believe, will always get you through some of your darkest hours and onto something greater, maybe even what you were destined for. Our hopes and dreams are served by our faith even as we confront overwhelming challenges in achieving them; it helps us to find the will to keep pressing on until we discover the solutions to our prob-lems or the course our lives ought to follow. I believe if we keep pushing forward, we will get through to better times as long as we trust our faith. Every persistent heart grows stronger muscles when its cells are infused with the power of personal faith and, I believe, a trust in God.

Think about the stresses we all encounter in the modern world. We can allow ourselves to be overcome with anxiety and fear and cre-ate situations that produce mental issues and even physical problems. There is real damage that can be done to ourselves if we don't find techniques for managing anxieties and fears about what comes next in our lives, or what we are dealing with daily. We can even create our own diseases and illnesses by making ourselves weak. I have been in very dif-ficult physical and emotional situations in my life, as we all have, and my utter confidence in my faith to sustain me made all the difference in how my problems were positively resolved. There are always times when the evidence makes it look like things will never improve and objects are insurmountable, but I have seen faith work for me and oth-ers that helped us to expect and even know we would see the arrival of good things. This was a conviction rooted in my heart and soul, and it has never left me.

There is also an increasing body of research on the impact of faith on people and how prayer and religious convictions improve our well-being. The data indicate that involvement with a supernatural "other" reduces loneliness and improves our immune systems. Those who include faith as a part of who they are report to sociologists that they feel better and healthier. There are even MRI results that indicate brain function displays while praying show that talking to a person's God is like speaking with a friend, which gives faith a social aspect. There seems to be no question that people who have an established relationship with God have worked very hard to make it a real part of their lives and emotionally uplifting, but I think there is also empirical evidence that faith as a personality trait, a strong belief in something greater than oneself, even without God as part of that equation, can be equally helpful for making our way in the world.

I do not mean to suggest to anyone that a life without faith is meaningless, or that faith requires a belief in a supernatural "other" or God. I only know that most of us are spiritual or identify with a religion, and that tends to have a positive effect in our lives and the lives of others, and we know the impacts of faith because they occur for everyone who relies on it. Many feel that without faith there is no meaning to our lives. I don't agree with that assumption. Anyone can be a good person, perform acts of kindness, and have made a conscious decision to make the world a better place and do all that without any kind of faith. The personal aspects of living a life of faith, though, are constantly talked about, and even researched. There are some indications that when people are very sick with deadly diseases, if they have strong faith, then they exhibit a better chance of healing and survival, and even have shortened times for healing.

By making faith one of my four pillars, I believe my life has been demonstrably improved. In some ways, it is like placing much of your life in the hands of destiny or God or the universe, and then having the confidence things will improve because of that external power. I am not sure I might have made it through the difficult times in my life were it not for my faith. Of course, I think it has made me a better person because faith keeps me caring and loving others and thinking about kindnesses I might offer. Mostly, though, it also gives me an internal kind of peace with which to live.

"We know that spirituality is something that really helps people feel like they find that higher power," said psychologist Jennifer Hartstein during a *CBS News* conversation. "They find that center, that groundedness, that can be anything for anybody. We know meditation, mindfulness, all those kinds of things can help change our brain chemistry, help us be less depressed, less anxious, and more centered, and that is good for all of us."

I think, also, it is important that people understand they don't just wake up one morning and experience profound faith. Living well and having faith is like any other endeavor and requires a constant awareness, and even a kind of practice of our faith. I see my faith everywhere in my daily life and, I believe, it is because I have learned to be mindful and conscious of its presence. All the personal characteristics we exhibit as adults tend to be acquired through learning and discipline, and I think acquiring a deep and abiding understanding of faith requires the same effort. When we take a moment to contemplate what faith might mean to us and how we can bring it into our lives, we might discover its importance and be grateful for what it can offer. We cannot, though, expect faith to roll over us like a revelation from above. We need to think, study, and prepare ourselves for an understanding that we previously might never have considered, because I am confident most people can make faith central to their lives if they try to comprehend its value and then put it into regular practice.

The Summit Mindset already requires that we do good where we can, and faith is elemental to that consideration, though it is not essential. We can get there alone without faith, but our task is much greater, the challenges more daunting without unwavering faith, and, for me, God. While researching various perspectives on faith, I came across the thinking of George Bernard Shaw, the Irish playwright who is one of only two people to win a Nobel Prize and an Oscar. His thinking reflects much of what I am trying to communicate on faith and happiness by offering up the tenets of my Summit Mindset.

"This is the true joy in life," Shaw wrote. "Being used for a purpose recognized by yourself as a mighty one. Being a force of nature instead of a feverish, selfish little clod of ailments and grievances, complaining that the world will not devote itself to making you happy. I am of the opinion that my life belongs to the whole community and as long as I live, it is my privilege to do for it what I can. I want to be thoroughly used up when I die, for the harder I work, the more I live. I rejoice in life for its own sake. Life is no brief candle to me. It is a sort of splendid torch which I have got hold of for the moment and I want to make it burn as brightly as possible before handing it on to future generations."

Which is a fine way for each of us to spend our precious time.

Exercise:

- **Exercise:** Think about the hardest times ever in your life. Do you remember how you reacted to an overwhelming problem? If you were strong and confident, what made you that way? Was it experience or faith? Do you think the hard times in your life would have been less painful had you exercised faith? What convinces you that there is a god who interacts with our lives? If you are a person of faith, think of the good things that came your way because of your faith and the strength it provides. Do you know people of great faith? How has it manifested in their lives? Faith is very private and individual to most of us, but can you offer a definition of faith for you and then point to examples of how it has manifested in your life?

CHAPTER EIGHT

COMMUNICATION

*The single biggest problem in communication is
the illusion that it has taken place.*

—GEORGE BERNARD SHAW

Everything we do in our lives, whether in business or personal interactions, is made more valuable and fulfilling with proper communications. My analysis is that the easiest and hardest thing we do as humans is communicate. Why is it difficult, though, to give someone detailed information and guidance to be more efficient at their jobs? Who are you not understanding because you don't listen well? What is the best way to communicate with employees or friends? Can you find a methodology to reach everyone with a mass communication, or do you need to speak to separate groups and individuals? How can you determine what is the best approach for communicating? Where, exactly, should you start to begin to improve your communications?

Any accomplishment I've had with any of the businesses I've led as an executive has always been built around an effective communications platform. I made no assumptions about what was happening internally regarding communications when I arrived at Essentia, but I was clear with our senior leadership teams that we could not accomplish our goals of increasing the value of the company and creating happy employees if we did not first get our communications practices right. Building a company culture for success did not matter if we were not communicating our values and goals across our employee groups and on to our vendors and customers. If we did that well, our staff would be engaged and motivated and would likely stay focused on what we had decided mattered the most to drive value. My job, too, as a leader, was to learn about our employees, their personal lives, and their roles in the company. The more I knew about everyone, the better I understood our operations and how to motivate people.

There are several different theories on communications and how they work best, and probably an endless list of what are considered best practices. When I developed the Summit Mindset, I wanted to refine communications techniques that would help people who were employing my ideas. These are protocols and practices I arrived at through years of managing people and companies. Communicating properly reinforces your business's North Star and the four foundational pillars you have laid out that define your company. I have found this works for individuals and organizations because it fortifies trust, possibly establishing it for the first time, and it acts as a galvanizing principle across any organization. Meaningful communications with a regular cadence that people can find dependable will make a company's journey toward its North Star real and executable. Consistency is critical, though. I am frequently surprised by leaders who fail to realize this essential element of business success. Because we live in an era where people can hide behind their screens and email templates, proper communication becomes incredibly important. The digital age requires us to be more diligent in our efforts to reach people within and without of our organizations and be mindful of not only what we are communicating but also how it is being communicated.

There are a surprising number of companies, including global brands, that have failed at this simple and important task of communication.

Nike, which was founded in 1971, has become an international sportswear brand that is almost universally recognized, but has still experienced communications stumbles. In 2018, a group of female employees conducted an anonymous survey to assess problems with what they viewed as a male-dominated culture at Nike's Beaverton, Oregon, headquarters. The findings indicated there was sexual discrimination and harassment of women in the workplace. One of the world's leading apparel brands was doing such a poor job with internal communications that it ended up being confronted by a rogue group of its own employees, who refused to continue tolerating their treatment. The CEO was forced to acknowledge he was unaware of the problems, which had also been caused, in part, by a lack of trust in the company's human resources departments.

Nike's problem might have been more than just a failure of diligence and oversight. The company grew so quickly that its demands for production and distribution outstripped any ability to establish an effective communications policy and infrastructure. The women's survey revealed there were wildly inefficient methods of bottom-up communications in house and that there was a disproportionate number of connections between management, but not staff. Corrections were made by implementing mandatory management training that turned the focus to a culture that was more inclusive and diverse. Several C-suite executives lost their jobs, while internal reporting processes and HR procedures were also overhauled.

When I arrived at Essentia, culture and communications were my initial focus. I had no real idea what was being accomplished with internal and external communications, but I knew they were both critical. Our vendors and distributors needed to know our goals and what was important to our brand, and employees would be more productive and engaged if we properly communicated what our company was about and the broader vision of Essentia. We became dedicated to a two-way communication that allowed leadership to learn from our employees and our vendors on what we might do better and how to improve operations, which also led to an increased revenue flow and people who were happier in their jobs. We built trust inside and outside of the company by being truthful and communicating information that had value and meaning, and it worked at Essentia just as effectively as it would have at any other company that had made the same commitment.

Zola Kane, our chief marketing officer at Essentia, was in a position to measure the impact of our rededication to better communications.

"I was actually more than a bit surprised," she said. "Of course, given my role, I knew it was important for my job. But what really amazed me was the way we all got better within the company at talking to each other across departments, making certain each group knew what the other was doing and how we might help facilitate their successes, and they could help us get our tasks accomplished for best results. I know how this might sound, but, honestly, we were a completely different company within ninety days. We were a part of something good before, but this was different, and we talked about it among ourselves and with our customers, and I just think that [communications] transformation changed performance by everyone. I think one of the things that happened, and it was fairly sudden, was that people started caring more about the company and each other, and there's just no way to put a value on that other than to say it can really be amazing."

My approach to begin refining communications at Essentia was to conduct weekly town hall–style meetings to hear employee issues and concerns, encourage positive stories and feedback, but also to establish standards of performance for the critical job of communicating. I thought this was an important first step in building a "people first" culture. My intention was to treat communications like every other business dynamic and measure it for performance, which means we began with a plan to use metrics. Essentia had to employ methods for measuring ROI on strategic and internal communications. This was not overly difficult. If our sales reps were given better collateral documents and increased the cadence with which they spoke to buyers of our products, we could easily compare sales figures with those from previous quarters. There were, of course, other factors that might influence improvement of those numbers, but much could be directly tracked back to better communications.

There was something more basic to what we were doing at Essentia, though. Good communications are a habit. Our town hall meetings became the place where we shared our progress and the smart actions that we were taking to complete mission critical projects. We adopted a fundamental philosophy of "say what we do and do what we say." Conversations were open and honest, and we asked the important, recurrent question, "What do we stink at?" When that was defined, the team set a course of action for improvement. I think when organizational cadence on communications is frequent, your path forward also becomes abundantly clear.

Our leadership team built an internal communications plan that spoke to the needs of our company. We could not do that without analyzing what was already in place and what was working and what was failing. When those questions were answered, we established goals for our communications to define what we wanted to accomplish, specifically internally. These do not all seem like big or obvious developments, but, for instance, we decided that all internal emails needed to be answered within a twenty-four-hour window. That single choice kept us communicating and acting every day. We also decided to show up five minutes early for every team call, which meant we got to the work before us immediately and did not wait on late participants. My goal was to keep our communications in motion because I knew it would lead to progress that would almost appear magical against any previous standards. People and organizations tend to feed off habitual communications. In one of our meetings, there was passing mention about helping the United Negro College Fund (UNCF), and an idea evolved to conduct a "virtual walk" to raise funds. Consistent communication on the concept led to the employee base of our small bottled water company becoming the top business contributor to UNCF in the Pacific Northwest.

Because we were not a large company, we had to be diligent about implementing the important measures for business improvement.

In my initial weeks at Essentia, I kept us focused internally, which is critical to small business performance. When that is mastered, we can look to external communications to let the market know what is new and different and better about our company, and how we can continue to improve. Twice weekly, I sent out a business update that talked about recent successes and identified opportunities, which led to our team landing a new national customer in a chain convenience store. Communication prompts growth and generates identifiable culture within a business. My belief is that the only real metric that matters to business results is daily communication combined with weekly recaps to constantly maintain awareness of progress. This is how any company and its employees become relentless competitors. Our people were empowered by communications, and many of our most significant accomplishments were achieved when no one was in the office because of the COVID virus.

What I had also learned through experience with the Summit Mindset was that we needed to keep our key messages consistent during both internal and external communications. Companies that did not have everyone telling the same story to all its constituent audiences often found themselves failing. Our goal was to provide all our employees with primary and secondary messages to deliver the important details on the company's mission and values. When your customers know you and your products and what you believe in—the principles and standards for corporate and personal citizenship—it becomes considerably easier, even natural, for them to purchase from you. Fairness, frequency, and consistency guided our communicators and offered a reassurance to internal stakeholders and not just our customers.

One other practice I wanted to make formal was the process of cross-functional, or cross-departmental, communications to improve efficiencies and collaborations. We established different methods for communicating between departments to help and learn from each other and pick up tips to create a better business. This connection between departments kept employees engaged with each other and avoided the feeling of isolation that often comes from laboring inside of a specialized silo. Our weekly town hall meetings became biweekly and turned into question-and-answer sessions where we learned of issues and picked up valuable information from leadership and fellow employees, much of which was later implemented to create a more productive and efficient operation. We also evaluated ourselves and our teams with a critical eye.

The Summit Mindset also requires transparency to be completely effective. In fact, we made transparency an integral part of our organizational thinking and found that it promoted an open dialogue, trust, and accountability. Our Essentia employees were made aware that leadership wanted them to feel comfortable asking questions and sharing their thoughts and ideas on anything related to the company. There was nothing more important to me than empowering our employees to feel they could contribute and make a difference. Not everyone learns all company information all the time, though. This is simply not possible, or needed, but maintaining a level of transparency on policies and practices is essential because it can directly affect an employee's work product. Transparency also allowed us to improve employee recognition. We used internal communications software to honor our achievers among their peers and let teams and individuals know they were appreciated and valued, especially when their contributions were critical to accomplishing certain goals. In fact, no other element of our efforts at Essentia maximized our growth and productivity more than transparency among employees and sustaining vibrant internal communications.

Communications also facilitate innovation. Even in a water company, you are operating a digital business, and transformation of processes can happen very fast. Every business needs to be adroit and able to quickly enact change, which is not possible without a strong communications platform. The bottled water industry is hypercompetitive, and I wanted to make certain our employees were all aware of our challenges and were constantly exchanging ideas to keep us improving against the other companies in our industry. If our workforce had been more widely distributed, those communications tools would have been more critical to performance. Regardless of the business type, in an age where people can be immediately reached with information, good and bad, on handheld devices, it is more crucial than ever that executives provide their employees with quality information to improve output and involvement with the company's culture and its goals.

Effective communications don't just facilitate the growth of companies; they can also save them from failure. Conversations can turn into tactics and strategies that solve problems and remedy mistakes. These types of transformations were demonstrated when Starbucks, the coffee company, ran into financial troubles because of its own bureaucracy and a downturn in the US economy. Profits had dropped by 28 percent between 2007 and 2008, and by 2009, the company had closed nine hundred stores and laid off 6,700 employees. Competition had also increased when outlets like McDonald's began to offer coffee bars that sold espresso.

The challenges to the Starbucks brand and its revenue prompted the board to bring back the company's early CEO, Howard Schultz, to reinvigorate the business and return it to the culture that had brought its initial success. He began his project with communications. The board chair, who was suddenly back as CEO, sent an email to every person in the company and took ownership of the ongoing failures. Schultz said it was wrong to blame the economy for Starbucks' slowdown because "heavy spending to accommodate expansion has created a bureaucracy that masked problems." Although the company was in forty-three countries with fifteen thousand stores and was serving fifty million customers a week in 2008, Schultz saw that his creation had to be shifted back to "customer-facing initiatives," which was a clear commitment to communication and connection.[8]

Schultz did not, however, hide behind an email template. When he ordered layoffs and store closures, he did it at a live company meeting where he stood before employees with a microphone and answered difficult questions.

---

8   Shezray Husain, Feroz Khan, and Waqas Mirza, "How Starbucks Pulled Itself Out of the 2008 Financial Meltdown," *Business Today,* September 28, 2014.

"People went after me," he told *Harvard Business Review* in a 2010 interview.[9] "I stood there and answered the questions, and I apologized for making decisions that people thought fractured the trust we had built for so many years. I tried to explain that these decisions were made on the basis of preserving the whole, and that I understood there would be damage. I also explained that we felt incredible compassion for the people who had to leave. You have to be honest and authentic and not hide. I think the leader today has to demonstrate both transparency and vulnerability, and with that comes truthfulness and humility and obviously the ability to instill confidence in people, and not through some top-down hierarchical approach. You must communicate."

Schultz remained convinced that what had made Starbucks successful was the element of community and the connections between the company's baristas and their customers. His original idea, which was to make the coffee experience a "third place" between work and home, had been lost with overheated growth and pressures to increase retail revenues at various storefronts. Immediately, he began to build an internal communications platform for employees to contribute ideas and strategies and have uninhibited conversations about the company and the challenges it was facing, with possible solutions. The employees, referred to as partners, had serendipitously provided a genesis for an idea to engage customers and accelerate Starbucks' transformation.

In just a few months after Schultz's return, Starbucks launched an interactive platform for two-way communications with its customers. The concept was called "My Starbucks Idea," and it enabled patrons to share their opinions with the company and each other regarding everything from Corporate Social Responsibility, advertising, brand image, products, services, and social media. Schultz was determined to rebuild customer relationships, and this first step was wildly successful with 1.3 million users on social media, who generated 5.5 million page views per month and 93,000 ideas. The company's customers realized they had a

---

9   Adi Ignatius, "The HBR Interview: We Had to Own the Mistakes," *Harvard Business Review* (July–August 2010), https://hbr.org/2010/07/the-hbr-interview-we-had-to-own-the-mistakes.

direct link to Starbucks management, and the changes instituted were an indication the leadership team was listening. More than one hundred of those ideas were implemented by the company, and brand trust was renewed. The community that Schultz had built the company upon was, in effect, being reborn and made stronger using digital media.

"There was great resistance inside to allowing the outside world to tell us what we are doing wrong," Schultz said in that same *Harvard Business Review* interview. "But the openness led to a different mentality. We weren't myopic about who we were and how we were going to go to market. We became more open and vulnerable, listened to people, and as a result, started creating a new methodology, a new language, and new tools and tactics that enabled us to become best of class."

Schultz and his leadership team recognized what he described as a "seismic shift" in how people access information and how that influences their behavior. Social media, he realized, made people want to feel they were sharing data instead of being given marketing materials. He described Starbucks customers and social media followers as being offered a "sense of discovery" that made them want to share information with someone they cared about. He assembled a team to design and implement digital and social media channels to make Starbucks a relevant and trusted source of information instead of a "promoter of products and ideas." Not only was there direct interaction with the people who used Starbucks products and stores, but also the cost of customer acquisition was dramatically reduced because there was almost no need to use traditional types of advertising. The strategy worked; Starbucks' Facebook page grew to thirty-six million Likes by 2022.

A significant contributing factor to Starbucks' ongoing growth after its slowdown was the early adoption of technology channels like mobile apps. These made it possible for the company to go directly to its online community and broaden its market by initiating a rewards program and a store locator, and offering new ideas that might become trends. The company used Twitter so well that by mid-2022 it had attracted more than eleven million followers. Direct lines of communication to that many customers on just Facebook and Twitter offer an almost incalculable advantage for selling directly and reducing the costs of outreach. These were even more important as Schultz began to institute changes such as acquiring a company that made a coffee-brewing system, a bakery chain, introducing an instant-coffee brand, and implementing various alterations to menu offerings.

Internally, though, Schultz drove communications with all the company's constituencies, from senior managers to store managers, analysts, media, partners, customers, and shareholders. The plan he kept repeating, and the process he wanted followed, was to share the company's vision, clearly lay out the plan for growth and a turnaround, foster two-way communications with partner employees and customers, and, perhaps most critically, let the employees know how they could help achieve these goals. This was a kind of organizational conversation that was being instigated by management, and it was transparent to enable the acquisition of valuable information from any source that could help.

Leadership makes other communications demands that are not about positive outreach. The CEO of a company tends to be the voice and face of a brand, and Schultz will be forever associated with his coffee company. He was board chair in 2018 when two Black men were arrested in Philadelphia for trespassing at one of Starbucks' stores. They had simply been waiting for a friend, and a call was made to the police by a White employee. Schultz, who stepped in front of the crisis to manage the company's message, acknowledged that "the reason the call was made is because they were African American." Protestors eventually showed up outside the store in Philadelphia, chanting, "Starbucks coffee is anti-Black." Schultz and CEO Kevin Johnson admitted their company's failure and closed eight thousand US stores several weeks later to train 175,000 employees on racial bias, which limited damage to Starbucks' brand image and undoubtedly increased internal awareness of potential racial biases by their partners. Communications skills and tools helped Starbucks deal with a crisis and to reimagine the company sufficiently to continue its growth trajectories.

There were two more high-profile incidents involving race that affected the Starbucks brand image. In California, a Black man in a store was asked to wait for his order outside because it was too crowded. He took note of the fact that he was the only Black person in the room while several White customers were lingering near the barista, waiting for their orders. Even when two White customers exited, he was yelled at to go outside. The incident, after what had happened in Philadelphia, was a negative that no company wants to experience. At another California store, a barista had scribbled the word *beaner* on a Hispanic customer's cup.

The return of Howard Schultz was about more than racial stumbles in his stores, though. Starbucks was trying to fend off a national trend toward unionization, which has reached into the giant company's employee population. He believes the issues are not with his company—because it has a reputation of providing reasonable pay and great benefits—but is a cultural failure of government and capitalism to enable a new generation of workers to succeed at levels they expect. Meanwhile, Schultz and Starbucks instituted a program to invest $1.5 billion in improving the company's policies regarding diverse vendors and to help increase opportunities in marginalized racial and economic communities, and he is using every communications skill at his disposal and all the digital tools available to spread the word that his company is something far greater than the sum of its mistakes.

My approach as CEO to avoid miscommunication about our company and its practices was to always be personal. I wanted to know the names of everyone who worked for me and learn as much about them as I could. An executive who knows their employees has a better ability to lead the company to success. This also applied to our vendors and customers. I felt the more I knew about the people who were directly connected to our financial success, the greater our ability to compete and win market share. While I have previously mentioned the importance of being a good listener, I think it is also critical that when you are interacting with someone, you must be fully present, not tapping your phone screen or looking down the hallway or across the room. Distractions need to be eliminated to give people your full attention to what they are saying. Turn off your phone. Close your laptop, listen, and be heard. Good communication is not complicated.

More important, of course, is what you are saying and to whom you are saying it. I arrived at my communications philosophy after decades of work and learning from many experts. Everyone in executive leadership roles has sat through media and communications training that is designed to make you more able to reach an audience or an individual. My conclusion is that simplicity makes for the best communications. And that a limited amount of information can be delivered. I think a company's brand and its core message needs to be kept to three basic statements. Whenever I spoke with an organization or a team, I identified the most important message I wanted delivered and emphasized that information, but I offered two more to complement the key message. I discovered, as did most researchers looking at communications best practices, that an audience or a single constituent or stakeholder can only remember one of those three points, which is why I make certain they understand their most important takeaway from every presentation or conversation. If someone can tell you a month later what your company's brand or your leadership style represents, then you have done your job as an effective communicator.

There is another important factor that often gets overlooked by leaders and communicators, and I've made it a key characteristic of the Summit Mindset. This is respect for the individual, their time and intellect and contributions to whatever may be the larger endeavor for a company or organization. I have always viewed it as my responsibility to return phone calls and emails and answer questions as quickly as reasonably possible. Responsiveness is an important trait for any executive or member of a leadership team, and it reflects on your philosophy as a businessperson or an individual when you treat others with respect. Being responsive is always appreciated and, invariably, leads to introductions and other referrals.

All the practices I have referred to thus far regarding communications are considerably more effective when they are delivered as part of a plan. I think every business needs to develop and execute against a strategic communications plan. That begins by examining what does and doesn't work and understanding goals for the company and the role played by communications. By defining business objectives for specific periods of time, a plan can be designed that effectively keeps your company on track toward those goals. These moves are as critical for external communications as they are for internal. Understand who is in your audience and create messaging that reaches them and addresses their concerns and solves their problems. Internally, the technology is almost as important as the messaging. Identify websites or programs that employees are inclined to use—for example, chat rooms, cloud services, and email templates that allow users to speak to specific relevant topics inside the company. These communications tools should be avenues for open and honest feedback from employees, demonstrating that the company has respect for their roles as representatives.

Success begins with an effective communications plan, and that plan starts with an audit of what the company is presently doing to reach the market and stakeholders in the business. There are often gaps in marketing messages or communications channels that are not reaching relevant audiences. These need to be identified and corrected as part of your new plan. You will need to gather and interpret data on what has been driving sales growth or brand image and compare that information with efforts that are not performing as well as desired. Your communications plan should always stay focused on a core message or two and who the people are that you want to hear what you have to say. Is it customers or employees or vendors? This may sound overly simple, but making the communications project complex can be a step toward also making it ineffective.

Begin with messaging. What are the messages you want to convey about your company and its products and services? Are they uniform for all stakeholders or customized based upon their place in the market or as shareholders? My experience is that the company needs a few key brand messages and then separate messages for whatever the company is selling, whether that is product lines or various services offered. A messaging platform, though, is essential for a successful business, and keeping employees focused on those messages makes aligning a communications plan with business goals considerably simpler to achieve. Use straightforward language and declarative sentences to state what your company or organization is about. Make it easy to understand what you offer and why your product or service is differentiated or unique from your competitors. Nuance is rarely effective in marketing.

Like the company itself, the communications plan must have goals. What do you want to accomplish? Is it something as obvious as "Raise sales by 10 percent every quarter of the current fiscal year"? Increased revenue is always a smart goal for any company, but the communications plan and its messages will need to be measured against whether the sales targets were met, and if they were not achieved, was it the communications plan that didn't work or was there another failure in the business infrastructure? Were there not enough sales conversations? Was 10 percent a realistic growth figure, or was the number too high and impossible to obtain in the economy of the time? Was the timeline for achievement too narrow? Be sure to ask questions that are relevant to all functionalities and not only the communications plan, but do not hesitate to reexamine the communications plan's effectiveness in helping financial accomplishments.

Nothing, of course, is more important than your audience. Who do you want to receive your messaging? Several communications channels will be employed, but who are the constituents and stakeholders you are targeting? A strong business brand will want to communicate its image and what it stands for, and that messaging will be for the broader marketplace, but what do you say to a retailer and its customers about the product you have on their shelves and why it is different and better than similar products that might be priced less? What makes your more expensive item worth the extra cost? If you can't communicate these distinctions, your company will suffer financially and not live up to its market potential. Do your shareholders and board members truly understand what you are trying to tell the world about your company? How are you reaching them and what are you saying? Are employees informed sufficiently so they can *live* the company brand, believe in the products or services, and know what to say to vendors, retailers, and consumers? Have you grown a culture that makes all that possible?

Communicating well is an art, but it's not just about what you say. The other factors include the forms of the media being used to send out your messages. The digital age has made it possible to reach constituent audiences with nicely produced videos or news releases with important links and graphic designs. You can also begin to build lists of customers or vendors and get them interested in company developments by using a newsletter format, produced regularly with a cadence that is not so frequent as to be annoying but often enough to keep them adequately informed. Remember that the messaging for each audience must be customized to their interests, which means a single email talking about a new product or a management hire needs to be framed by your communications team in a manner that makes it relevant to that specific group of readers.

My belief also is that every company, whether in the growth stage or as a multinational corporation, needs a crisis communications plan. Hopefully, this is a document that is never used but is on a shelf, physically or digitally, and is ready if the worst should happen to your company. The elements of such a plan ought to include a methodology for quickly developing responsive messaging that speaks directly to the issue causing the crisis. These messages might be sent to internal stakeholders like investors and partners, but if the crisis has emerged in the marketplace and the public is aware of a problem like a flawed or contaminated consumer product, a broader approach is required. Mitigating a crisis with an effective and well-executed communications plan can save a company from obsolescence.

When communicating about your company's crisis, honesty is essential. The entirety of my Summit Mindset is built on a foundation of honesty and truthfulness, and I have found that it is the only approach anyone should ever take in operating a business or communicating with other parties of interest. I am no expert on managing crises, but I do understand the importance of transparent communication and honesty, and there is apparent logic to be shared regarding a crisis. The first step is to admit what happened. Was it an honest mistake? Did a design flaw do harm to a consumer? Was a purchase made to save money in manufacturing that turned into a product failure? Are you employing someone who should not have been a part of your company and they acted improperly? Were third parties involved in a failure that impacted your company?

After the cause of your crisis has been discovered, the next task is to let your customers, vendors, and stakeholders know what happened. Avoid pointing fingers or assigning blame. Make certain the explanation to all stakeholders is easy to understand and placed in the context of improbability that defied the odds. Nothing is more important, however, than your apology to every group from investors to consumers. A business that fails in a manner that harms its customers must offer a sincere apology and explanation. Depending on the issue, my belief is that management ought to use local or national media to clarify the problem and make certain the apology shows the acceptance of responsibility. The public tends to be very forgiving and, generally, willing to provide second chances.

What's next? Fix the problem that caused the crisis. If it is a flaw in product assembly, make a correction. A food processor might have to change how its products are kept safe and free of bacteria. Manufacturers of aircraft, obviously, must abide by full disclosure after crashes caused by a mechanical failure. There is a different process for every business when its lapses go public, but whatever has happened, the leaders must then explain how that problem has been repaired and the company has been improved. The information on improvement must also be persuasive, and, if possible, demonstrated. Ultimately, in terms of brand image and reputation of the business and its products, the executive team must accept responsibility for what happened on their watch and be convincing that such a thing will never again happen or cause harm.

The responsibility for communicating during those difficulties belongs to the CEO or a founder still in an executive or management role. A company's reputation and image are built not only around products and services and the quality delivered to the market, but also on the character and performance of the senior executive, which almost always ought to be the CEO. A CEO standing before TV cameras and offering honest answers to tough questions from journalists, conducting themselves with confidence and understanding, will have the most significant impact on mitigating any crisis. Customers and investors will take you at your word, but they will also expect you to manage the crisis in a way that will bring it to an end and leave the company a chance to continue growing and profiting. The credibility of the leadership creates the credibility of the company.

Wells Fargo Bank did almost the exact opposite of what I have just described. Company executives sent out communications that the financial institution wanted to grow and needed new accounts. Quotas were established, and managers at the local branches felt the only way to reach the unrealistic demands was to set up two million fake bank accounts in the names of existing customers without their consent. The Consumer Financial Protection Bureau was tipped to the fraud, an investigation was begun, and the bank was issued a $185 million fine. That, however, was only the beginning of their troubles.

Because of an evasive strategy regarding the allegations, Wells Fargo, a legacy institution dating back to the early days of the US, is in possession of a diminished brand. The executive management of the company failed and even refused to apologize, while also trying to characterize the claims as not that widespread or harmful. In fact, Wells Fargo failed to take any responsibility. Months after the fraud was discovered, the CEO was called to testify before the US Senate's Banking Committee, and only then did he issue an apology that acknowledged what had happened during his tenure. There were also indications the CEO knew trouble was brewing because he sold $61 million of his personal stock the month before the investigation was launched. Further, instead of accepting responsibility, Wells Fargo leadership blamed 5,300 staff employees who were mostly clerks and low-level accountants and salespeople. They were all fired.

Fixing the Wells Fargo mess would not have been easy, but it ought to have been attempted. There was no real proactive response to the crisis, and the failure to communicate left the trust broken with their customers and the public. In fact, there was no issuance of a general apology to consumers or the marketplace, nor were there any indications the company ever accepted responsibility. If the executive leadership team had been forthright and admitted they had failed, they might have been able to talk about policies and procedures that could have been implemented to ensure no such fraudulent activity might ever take place again, but that didn't happen either.

If you have a business and you want to reach or remain at the summit, you will need to conduct other specific forms of communications. There is little chance of the kind of success you likely envision without undertaking marketing communications, often referred to as MarCom. This is a broad range of tools used to narrowly focus your messaging to target markets. This is different from public and media relations, which reach out more widely and seek to communicate directly with customers or other interested parties who can grow your market size and revenue. Conduct even a small amount of research to determine who your most likely buyers and current customers are, and ask them specifically why they are buying your products and services and how they solve their problems. The more you understand your target market's needs and visions for their companies, the better you can sharpen your communications strategies to reach those potential buyers. Do the work necessary, though, to identify your key markets to avoid ending up with strategies and communications that do not work.

To make your MarCom efforts have the greatest impact, you ought to have already worked out your brand message and differentiators. Customers need to know why they ought to buy your products instead of a competitor's. This effort needs to be focused on positioning your brand as the best in your industry with a simple, clarifying message. Give a potential customer an accessible reason to choose your company over their other options. Deciding what you want your brand to communicate to customers and the wider world is not always easy. If it is within your budget, consider using a focus group or various types of surveys with questions that give you feedback on current perceptions in the marketplace about your competitors, and even your products and services. Find out what the market's opinion is of your brand and what makes it strong and distinctive, and then build messaging around those characteristics.

The next step, obviously, is getting out the marketing messages. Even for start-ups, there are now various channels that serve to reach specific audiences. The internet, however, is crowded, and there is much white noise; to be effective, you must spend your time and resources wisely. Websites need to be calibrated for Search Engine Optimization (SEO) and the effective use of key words to move pages up on indexes, but increasingly, even start-ups are investing in search engine marketing (SEM). The purchase of ads on relevant social media and through Google and Bing increase exposure to audiences, which can all be targeted based upon demographics you are hoping to reach. Blogs, email marketing, and social media are all affordable methods of reaching targeted markets, though a consistency of effort is critical. If, as the Summit Mindset recommends, you do the reps consistently, I am confident your company will begin to experience traction.

What, exactly, does doing the reps mean regarding marketing communications? Marketing effectively requires consistency. Posting to a blog or sending out an email to a curated database a few times a month is not likely to achieve your goals of growth. New content is needed more frequently. Search engine algorithms do not like old material. If you haven't posted to a blog in over a month, chances are good that your website has not shown up in an index that will get you discovered, unless someone is directly searching for your product or site. Write new pieces for your blog, which should be linked on your business pages, and do it as often as time permits. Two or three posts a week will increase your marketing exposure. Remember that just a two-hundred-word blurb will enhance the odds of increased search engine exposure because it delivers new language to the bots running on the web. Find a cadence for your MarCom materials that works and that your company can maintain. Offer market insights and expertise, but when possible, be *newsy* regarding developments at your company. Concentrate on providing information the market might not get from other sources. The more knowledgeable your communications are, the stronger your brand image.

With a plan and infrastructure in place, the next step is to execute against your goals. Not much matters, either, without metrics to determine how you are doing with your marketing communications. The easiest metric to track tends to be website traffic. After you have launched your MarCom campaign, look at the site's visitation rates and how long people are staying on your pages. Figure out which pages get the most traffic and go back to look at the links or communications that led them to your site. What do you consider a reasonable goal for traffic increase? If you only spent a few thousand dollars to get your campaign running, web traffic jumped by 10 percent, and 3 percent of those visitors converted to customers, chances are good your investment in MarCom has yielded profitable results. What do page views look like, and do site visitors have a chance to interact with your company? Are you effectively dropping them into a sales funnel and generating new leads? These are all metrics that can tell you if your messaging is working and whether you chose the right channels for sending out marketing communications.

Public and media relations are also essential parts of your marketing strategy. They are simply designed for a broader audience. In fact, they add legitimacy to your company and brand. When a third party, maybe a reporter, discovers what you are offering and writes about your product, you have the kind of affirmation that cannot be delivered by your own efforts. This *earned media* adds credibility to your company because it is written by an outsider. Smart, in-house media relations professionals make that happen by pitching stories to reporters at vertical publications and websites and developing relationships to get ideas in front of journalists who write about your space. Writing and distributing news releases to various wire services, local papers, and broadcast media increase the odds that industry and mainstream writers who are always looking for stories will find your company and consider it worthy editorial content. Make sure that story pitches include quotes from relevant executives and even designers or innovators working at your company so the journalists can have a sense of what type of person they will be interviewing and the kind of quotes, provocative or insightful, they can expect to publish in their stories. Don't scare them off with manufactured controversies, but avoid being bland and institutional with your communications. Be sure to look for reporter bylines on recent stories that are topical to your industry and that might be relevant to what you are selling.

None of this is complicated. It is about execution. Remember, you are basically picking your message, deciding what medium to use, and then delivering to a targeted audience. Those are strategic choices, but they include numerous options: private messaging on sites like LinkedIn, direct messages on Instagram, or simple Facebook ads that are geofenced around the community where you work, sell, and live. Also, consider a TikTok feed or a basic YouTube channel, and explore video ideas that attract attention and build credibility and interest for a wider audience. Spend some time on alignment, though, before you go to the market. Make certain your brand aligns with the customers you've identified who will want your products and services, and that the overall approach fits your budget. Keep the customer first. Understand what they want, how their needs and interests are changing, and then build your communications and MarCom strategies around their environments. Their best interests, ultimately, serve your company's best interests. Experiment and find the right mix of selling, public relation events, brand influencers, sponsorships, and content creation. Add or subtract elements like Facebook and Google Ads with potential print media and sales promotions. There is almost certainly a formula that will work for your company's growth and success.

Remember, the Summit Mindset teaches that success starts with an Inside-Out job. We look at ourselves and our best characteristics for accomplishment, but we also focus on what we stink at because by confronting that and improving our skills, we increase the odds of building a winning business. When the foundation of improved and more capable "self" has been established, our next task becomes an Outside-In process. By looking outside of the company and yourself, you begin the study and understanding of the market. Knowledge of what the market needs gives you a better idea of how to launch your business. Begin taking *smart actions* that you define, and understand how they will help your company and you, as recommended by the Summit Mindset. Ask yourself continually what you are doing, and what your purpose is as a person and a business. Keep pressing and you will make the kind of progress that is life changing in the battle of You versus You. Stay humble and hungry on your journey.

And always remember, there is no finish line.

Exercises:

- **Build a Company Culture:** Begin talking regularly about how you will build a *people first* culture at your business. Share examples of servant leadership. Is there someone in your company who is actively involved in giving back to the community? What can you learn together as a group from their example? Create the expectation of communication across the entire team. How do you make certain everyone understands it is their responsibility to be an example and communicate? Work together to define what a great culture would look like at your company. Find examples of how you can improve as a company by reviewing failures. How do you improve? Constantly ask each other what you stink at while also celebrating victories.

- **Write a Marketing Communications Plan:** If you have a business or a product, draft a marketing communications plan to grow your revenue and brand awareness. Identify your best audiences and the channels to use to make the plan effective. Now determine your message. What do your target markets want to hear from you about your product? Can you find a single sentence or two that clearly states why you are different from competitors and are better able to provide your customers with an affordable solution? Create a story pitch for your company. Is there something topical in business news that might be relevant to your company's offering? Think of a way to insert yourself into those conversations. Search reporters' bylines to see if you can find someone who has written about your industry. What would you say to them to get their interest? How do you reach that reporter? What is the hook you want to offer that journalist about your product or company?

CHAPTER NINE

THE PURSUIT OF HAPPINESS

Happiness is a direction, not a place.

—SYDNEY J. HARRIS

They were three old men, but they had the broad smiles of someone young seeing a bright tomorrow of adventure and happiness. Each of them was staring at a canoe loaded with gear and about to be slid down a muddy bank into a Texas river. They were probably recalling memories of the first time they had stood at that riverbank and contemplated a fantastic journey. Fifty-four years earlier, during the Great Depression, they had made a capricious decision about canoeing the Texas Colorado River from the arid source of its headwaters all the way to the Gulf of Mexico. Jim Pickard's parents had an old canoe hanging on hooks in their garage, and when his pals Winfield James and Harry Caldwell saw it gathering dust on the wall, someone, they can't remember who, suggested they make sandwiches, fill some water jugs, and start paddling the six hundred miles toward Matagorda Bay.

"We didn't think much about it at the time," Winfield told a TV reporter. "We just thought it might be adventurous and we could have some fun. There wasn't an awful lot to be happy about back in that time. We sure didn't think it through very well, though. To be honest, I think maybe we were just trying to get out of having to get summer jobs. The country was coming out of the Depression back then, remember."

The only thing they had planned was their destination. The three eighteen-year-olds became a national sensation as they made their way down the river, and the Associated Press filed stories about their progress. People living along the Colorado offered them food and shelter, and they did not go without during their journey. A little over three weeks later, they arrived at the Gulf on the shores of Matagorda Bay and earned a little piece of Texas history when they were named after their hometown as "the Abilene Boys" by reporters. Tired, burned by the relentless Texas sun, they had never been happier, and over a half century later, they wanted to again make their epic trip.

"Well, I know everyone thinks we're crazy at this age to be doing something like this," Jim Pickard said as he tossed gear into the waiting boat. "But no matter what your age, you gotta do things that excite you and make you happy. That's what we're doing. We've hardly gotten to see each other through all these years, and now here we are acting like teenagers again. Can you think of what's wrong with that?"

Their lives had been distinctly different. Winfield James had left Texas for the big city and become the publisher of the *New York Daily News*, while Harry Caldwell stayed in their hometown and opened a successful music store. Jim Pickard chose nuclear physics and was employed working on the Manhattan Project at Los Alamos Laboratories in New Mexico. Knowing what they wanted out of life seemed to be a unifying characteristic of the Abilene Boys, and they were not fearful of being in their midseventies and paddling a canoe to the Gulf. The risk was worth the return in joy and adventure.

"Well, wish us luck," Winfield said.

He looked over at the TV cameras, reporters from around the region, and local officials and waved before he pushed the boat and then jumped in the back to steer Harry and Jim and him into the open current. They surely must have had some concerns about their physical abilities and whether they could handle rapids and the heat, but no worries were expressed. The only abundant emotion was happiness, and the river carried them gently away from the assembled crowd in the first stretch toward their destination.

Hearing the story of the Abilene Boys made me wonder again about what constitutes happiness. What is it? I know that may sound like a profoundly foolish question, which has baffled thinkers for all human history, but go ahead and try to give yourself an answer. Don't we all define happiness differently? Maybe it's a dream job traveling the world or meeting the person with whom we want to share our lives. I think it's reasonable to claim that most people associate happiness with money and having enough of it to be independent and live their lives however they please. There is, of course, a dictionary definition of happiness, but it is uniquely inadequate: "Happiness is an emotional state characterized by feelings of joy, satisfaction, contentment, and fulfillment. While happiness has many different definitions, it is often described as involving positive emotions and life satisfaction."

The definition is accurate enough but incomplete. We tend to think of happiness as an achievable and constant state, but it is almost always transitory. The amount of happiness each of us experiences has much to do with how capable we become at cultivating it, managing our perspectives through the time and tides of our lives. My sense is that people have a great tendency to view happiness as a goal, but it is not. I have led my life overwhelmingly happily by viewing it as a process. We spend too much time thinking about what we need to make us happy. I read that there is now a new psychological condition being discussed that relates to people spending their time on real estate sites looking for a new or better home. They are convinced that if they can just discover the perfect home, make a good deal, and move, then the rest of their lives will be happy. I know many individuals who view happiness as a finish line, a belief that if certain things happen, then they will finally get to be happy and that will be a continuous state, which is an idea I find almost ridiculous. What happens to them, though, in the interim when they are experiencing life's peaks and valleys and varied emotions? Can they not find happiness on the roller coaster we all ride?

There are few subjects that have been written about and discussed more than happiness. Every thinker from the ancient Persians to the Greeks and Romans and modern psychologists, psychiatrists, and sociological researchers have all been trying to grasp what it means to be happy, and how to arrive at such an attractive destination. The term modern experts use as a kind of catch-all for the topic is *subjective well-being*, which centers on an individual's overall feelings about their present life condition. This means that the person generally experiences more positive than negative feelings and moods, and they are satisfied with various parts of their lives that include work, relationships, and achievements. Their subjective impression or belief is that they are happy. One of those ancient philosophers I mentioned, Aristotle, argued that happiness was the only true human desire and that every other desire we have exists only to help us achieve happiness. He believed that happiness was the central purpose of human existence, and he spent countless hours contemplating and writing and teaching about that essential goal.

Aristotle's basic understanding of human happiness is relevant today after more than 2,300 years of advancing science and thought. In his lectures and notes from his time, the philosopher insisted that happiness was the product of the exercise of virtue. He concentrated happiness on the development of character and virtues like justice, prudence, benevolence, temperance, and courage. Happiness for rational humans, he believed, was only achievable through the perfection of those virtues. Accomplishing that mortal goal requires intellectual contemplation, which, according to Aristotle, provides the ultimate perfection of our natures through rational reflection. By his standards of thinking and interpretation of human behavior, he believed that happiness was a goal, not a temporary state, and that it cannot truly be achieved until the end of our lives. Aristotle called happiness the ultimate end and purpose of human existence.

Does this mean we don't experience happiness as the years of our lives unfold? If I were a philosopher instead of a businessman, I might ask Aristotle, "What is the point of happiness if it does not come until the end? Can't we be happy before we are old and lying in our death beds and taking a full measure of our lives?" We all know the answer to that query. Yes, we can enjoy happiness along the way. The follow-up question is how we acquire happiness prior to the end of our lives. I expect the emotion we feel at the end of a life well lived is more about contentment with our effort and not happiness as we lie dying. We are all going to experience a range of emotions from sadness to boredom and anger, frustration, and loneliness, but how do we remain happy through life's complexities? Truly happy people are confident of future happiness even when they are faced with these types of discomforts. They are sustained by a sense of optimism that things will get better, regardless of their present condition or circumstance.

I thought, in so many ways, the story of the Abilene Boys doing a reprise of their trip down the Texas Colorado after a half century was a perfect metaphor for life and the pursuit of happiness. They were certain to encounter problems—not only because of their age—and wonder why they had decided to make such a trip so late in life. But then the temperatures would cool, even as the sun came out, and three old friends would be together amid beautiful surroundings with no obligation other than enjoying their very existence. They were not on the river for more than several days, unfortunately, until they met their first problem. Harry, who had been dealing with early signs of Alzheimer's disease, became unable to communicate normally or help with tasks. His family came to retrieve him, but his boyhood friends, who were devastated by his departure, elected to continue toward the Gulf.

Were the two remaining Abilene Boys still able to pursue happiness, or were they simply grinding out a task they had set for themselves? Surely they were enjoying the journey, though they almost certainly missed Harry and, perhaps, they began to question whether the absence of the third hand to share the rowing might affect their progress or overall success. I wondered if their definition of happiness changed when they hit that first hard part of their adventure. I doubted it.

I do know that when I started thinking about the Summit Mindset, I began considering the meaning of happiness and how it can be acquired. Obviously, I had no formal professional training, but I encountered a broad range of people and had experiences that kept informing me about an approach and what mattered to everyone. I wondered if there were some commonalities among happy people. Did they have a certain type of personality to make them naturally happy? Did they start out in their lives with a safety net of family money? Was it an abundance of friends or a closeness to nature? Were their relationships deeper and more meaningful than casual associations? I was looking for something I could grasp on to and learn from regarding happiness and if I might be able to offer an insight or a protocol in the Summit Mindset.

I wanted to keep things simple, but the more I learned, the more I came to understand that happiness had been dissected and deconstructed to the point that it was broken down almost into elements. Psychological studies had identified two main types of happiness that related to pleasure and meaning. Experiencing enjoyment, feeling a sense of satisfaction, taking care of yourself, fulfilling your desires, and just doing what feels good are the forms of *pleasure* happiness. The other category is about having a sense of meaning. People who experience this kind of happiness feel that their lives have value, purpose, and meaning. This is probably derived from Aristotle's idea of the exercise of virtues to achieve happiness. You acquire it in this classification by investing in and accomplishing long-term goals, finding ways to fulfill your responsibilities, expressing concern for the welfare of other people, and living up to your own standards and personal ideals. A third type of happiness often added to discussions and studies is described as engagement, which involves feelings of participating and committing to various endeavors in our lives. Someone who is involved in building a home for Habitat for Humanity, for instance, is much more likely to feel happy than a person sitting on the couch and watching reruns and eating chips.

If you do even the slightest amount of research, you quickly discover that happiness, maybe next to religion, is the most discussed topic in humankind's history. Every culture has parables and stories about achieving happiness. The advice is unlimited and often contradictory, though much of it is helpful. The grossest oversimplification of the topic, I think, is when people are told they can simply choose to be happy. Imagine how insulting such advice might be if you lost your job, your home was foreclosed upon, your car was repossessed, and you were living on the street with your spouse and four children. Sure, just choose to be happy and everything will be fine. While happiness is, in fact, a state of mind and is partly a reflection of attitude toward life, it isn't a product that is simply pulled from a shelf. I have found that we need to develop our happiness, almost as we do our other skills, even muscles.

The hardest fact for us to accept about happiness is that it is synthetic, which means either we create it for ourselves or we don't. A study by Northwestern University in recent years reported that people with sustaining happiness can acquire it through habitual behaviors. The data shows that event-based happiness, something like winning the lottery, is transitory and that individuals with those big moments are no happier than the rest of us living lives that lack such dramatic events. Money and material things are clearly not a magic formula for happiness. Instead, developing habits that we perform regularly in our lives is the best way to become happy. The Northwestern researchers listed several habits shared with them by people who considered themselves happy, and they are worth your consideration. You will find several of these familiar as part of the Summit Mindset, and adopting a few can lead to a dramatic change in your attitude and create happiness.

1. **Remain Positive:** Even when bad things happen to happy people, they make themselves reflect and concentrate on what they are grateful for. Pessimism is the greatest enemy of happiness, even when it might be justified by circumstance. There is a great risk that it becomes a self-fulfilling prophecy and the worst happens, which makes happiness unlikely. Usually pessimism is

illogical, and when we force ourselves to look at the facts, we frequently find a solution to our immediate problem, execute that solution, and then get on with our lives.

2. **Try to Be Happy:** Happiness isn't a muscle, but like many good things in our lives, it does require effort and even training. We can easily slip into a routine where we fail to pay attention to our emotions and make no effort to focus on the happy and positive. Stay aware of your moods, and make decisions that keep happiness in mind. Supremely happy people work hard every day to get that feeling.

3. **Keep a Growth Mindset:** People with a growth mindset are convinced they can improve their lives by trying. A fixed mindset means you accept who you are and that you cannot change, which leaves little opportunity for making your life better or experiencing more happiness. Individuals who believe in personal growth and focus on their self-improvement generally outperform people with a fixed mindset because they embrace challenges and view them as opportunities to learn something new.

4. **Help Others:** I mentioned this as one of the four pillars of my life using the Summit Mindset. There may be nothing more important in our lives. The person you help will become happy, and you will have a surge of good feelings that scientists say are created by chemicals in our body when we do good. A Harvard group said that their work showed employees who helped others were ten times more likely to be focused on their jobs and 40 percent more likely to be given a promotion.[10] People who were committed to helping others were also shown to be the most likely to be happy even as they experienced times of stress. Spend money on other people, too, even if it is a small, inexpensive gesture. Every

10   Melanie Curtin, "Harvard Research Says You Are 40 Percent More Likely to Get a Promotion If You Do This 1 Thing," *INC,* June 9, 2019, https://www.inc.com/melanie-curtin/harvard-research-says-youre-40-percent-more-likely-to-get-a-promotion-if-you-do-this-1-thing.html.

time you do this, and make someone feel special or happy, you discover it is much better than spending money on yourself.

5. **Get Adequate Sleep:** I have never felt happier or performed better in my life than when I am getting enough sleep. Our moods, self-control, and focus are all more well managed, and energy levels are maximized to improve attention and memory. Being deprived of appropriate amounts of sleep also creates stress hormones in your body even if there is no external stressor present in your day. Think of your brain as the battery to your computer, and when you have sufficient sleep, your battery will be fully charged and able to perform all its tasks.

6. **Exercise:** I find this to be as important as sleep when it comes to helping make me happy. Of course, good exercise leads to good sleep, and when it is the type of exercise you enjoy, you are more than doubly fulfilled. Our brains and our muscles are soothed by exercise, and we also can better control impulse behaviors. Schedule your exercise; don't make it optional. Be intentional, and then follow through on the commitment. I can almost guarantee your mood will improve after a good workout, whether it's running, swimming, weights, cycling, or a treadmill. Exercise becomes a kind of magic that helps bring us happiness.

7. **Good People:** Nothing creates happiness as well as other happy people. You will find your confidence and creativity increase when you are interacting with happy friends, colleagues, and family. Happiness begets happiness just as negativity begets negativity. Avoid pity parties of individuals who want to feel sorry for themselves. Help them, if you can, but don't let them splash their mud on your psychological shoes. Stay close to happy people, and it will be easier for you to become and stay happy.

8. **Smell the Roses:** Simple advice, but powerful. Don't just hurry past beauty—stop and take it in. Shake up your routine. Have an amazing conversation; skip the small talk and gossip. Connect

with someone on a deeper and more emotional level to create a meaningful relationship. Indulge in an exquisite meal, wait for a dark sky and stare at the stars, and appreciate the mysteries of the universe. Everyone needs to slow down and savor life, regardless of how effective your routines are in getting tasks accomplished.

Pursuing happiness also requires a certain amount of caution. Individuals hoping to become happy but unable to experience the feeling might end up even more sad or depressed than prior to their decision to seek out happiness. You can chase happiness away if you go after it too hard, and if you expect to be happy every single moment of your life, disappointment becomes inevitable. What if you end up happy but wonder why you have spent emotional energy in pursuit of a goal that was not as satisfying as you had hoped? Searching for happiness, never knowing precisely what it means to you and not quite finding it, or getting there and not recognizing it, can lead to a surprising unhappiness, and maybe even sadness. American philosopher Eric Hoffer said bluntly, "The search for happiness is one of the chief sources of unhappiness."[11] The concept is so important to Americans, though, that our country was founded, in part, with the Declaration of Independence proclaiming we had a right to the "pursuit of happiness." More than two and a half centuries later, the World Health Organization said the US, the richest country on earth, was also the most anxiety-ridden and that a third of Americans will deal with a significant anxiety problem during their lifetimes.

So, what are we doing wrong?

I'm not sure happiness is something that can simply be *found*. Perhaps the more reasonable idea is that it can be devised by you to fit your character and life. The approach might almost be considered clinical, but there are various steps we can take to move us closer to enjoying as much happiness as is available in our circumstances. Carole Pertofsky, MEd,

---

11   Eric Hoffer, *The Passionate State of Mind and Other Aphorisms* (Chutchogue, New York: Buccaneer Books, 1955), 151.

Stanford Director Emerita, health promotion services and lecturer, School of Medicine, suggests there are methods to shift our mindsets to "better handle disappointments and obstacles" and that will allow us to "cultivate more joy and meaning in each day."[12] One of her recommendations is to do what we can to mitigate stress and disappointment. Pertofsky even recommends that we talk to ourselves as we would a child or a dear friend, neither of whom we would speak to negatively. She believes that self-forgiveness and self-compassion will move us closer to happiness and help us pass more quickly through difficult times.

Pertofsky offers several logical steps to increase the odds of achieving happiness. These include making ourselves aware of the origins of negative thinking. We are wired through evolution, she explained, for our brains to scan for dangers and threats, but we are capable of a kind of reset. The mindset she talks about is to develop mindfulness and kindness, learn to savor the good, and accept that difficulties are a part of living. Acceptance of disappointment and discomfort becomes the first step to returning to happiness. She reminds people to focus on peace, joy, or just practical optimism that will transform distress and move us toward gratefulness. We can then begin to recover, correct our mistakes, and even offer ourselves and others forgiveness, which frees us from being trapped in anger and hurt over things we simply cannot control.

As I continued to work at various jobs and learn about people and processes and, yes, happiness, I began to think I knew what happiness was about for me. I started formulating the Summit Mindset and came to the realization that everything I was offering was connected to happiness. Yes, there are elements of what I am recommending that speak to professional fulfillment and friendships, but those are also a part of finding happiness. Eventually, I concluded that my life, and I think most other lives, are about chasing happiness, which prompts the question of the definition of the word. My belief, arrived at after years of experience, reading, and contemplation, is that we find happiness by being a part of something greater than ourselves and making a meaningful contribution to that effort. For most of us, this is through our jobs and the work we do daily. Happiness in our work is having a voice, being heard, and contributing to a greater good. I think that is the most reliable and continuously fulfilling source of happiness for most people. I understand the advice that suggests chasing happiness can lead to frustration and even sadness for failure to catch that which you have been pursuing. The alternative, though, is to simply not try, and isn't happiness a goal worth running after and trying to experience?

Work, I believe, gives most of us purpose, and purpose is what provides happiness. We don't, however, need to find purpose in a job that pays our bills. There are other approaches to finding happiness. People find purpose in doing work for others or creating art; maybe they are driven to improve educational opportunities for underserved children in their hometown. In these kinds of scenarios, the work you do to pay the rent is different than the work that fills your soul. Many people deal with this contradiction, but when it is in service to personal happiness, there hardly seems any difficulty involved.

Whether we acknowledge it or not, though, we spend our lives chasing happiness. We also use much of our time working, which means it is important to find employment that is meaningful and then do it well. Work, frankly, is what makes most of us feel alive and have value. It gives us purpose, and it's not only about the money. I also peg individual happiness to self-reflection and asking the tough question I mentioned previously as part of the building blocks of the Summit Mindset: "What do I suck at?" The more we seek to find ways for self-improvement, the greater our joy at performance, and we will have an increased sense of valued contribution. This is the ultimate resolution to the conflict of You versus You. Having an honest self-evaluation of our strengths and weaknesses as employees and people, then finding methods to make improvements will help us reach our potential on the job and in our personal relationships.

We make a mistake when we consider happiness a constant state or a destination at which we arrive and everything in our lives becomes permanently joyous and beautiful. Life, of course, is nothing like that. Our emotions require context and perspective. The sun tends to look and feel brighter after a long, cold rainfall. We need to ask ourselves why we are happy at any given moment. Have I contributed at work or at home to make others happy? If I am miserable, what I can give to others usually isn't of much value. I need to constantly try to understand what sets my soul up to be purposeful and successful, and then never let myself be satisfied. Maybe that's not achieved through my job where I draw a paycheck. The formula for happiness for me might involve finding a way to improve the world or help people, and I will work a job that makes it possible for me to live the life I want in my hours away from the office. I know, also, that happy people are not complacent. They are moving in a desired direction to accomplish various goals. They want to improve and do better on whatever is their task. I think *satisfied* is a terrible state. I believe humans are meant to be stimulated, and that happens with work and empowerment and real purpose and contributing ideas and energy to the greater good, whatever we personally decide that might be.

I do not want anyone to get the impression that the Summit Mindset is about working your life away to the point you cannot be happy without your job. I have found, however, that because work is such a central part of our lives, we need to find a job or a career that gives us additional meaning by contributing to the larger vision. This doesn't mean that you don't take happiness from being with your family and friends, taking a quiet walk along the river or a dream vacation, or any of life's other pleasures. I am saying, though, that work gives us purpose, and a purpose is critical for us to achieve happiness, even when that purpose is outside of the work that we do to make living affordable and support our families. Being a contributing part of a team that is working toward a business goal or a nonprofit that is trying to feed or house people are both examples of how work fulfills us, gives our lives meaning, and renders happiness into our days.

Religions and other belief systems tend to be focused on happiness or types of enlightenment with the belief that by being enlightened, one becomes happy through an understanding of existence. Enlightenment for religions generally means reaching an unshakable faith in a God, which will then bring happiness and understanding of existence and your place in the world. Often, this involves embracing who you are and what you are doing, regardless of its relative importance to you. Zen Buddhists believe meditation on these topics will lead to enlightenment because true enlightenment can only be achieved through the profound realization that one is already an enlightened being. Using a koan, which is a question or paradoxical statement, the Zen approach is to provoke great doubt. This is to test or create practice for a student's progress in becoming Zen.

One of the best known koans is interpreted to be about the value of work, regardless of the chore. In the story, a novice who is trying to become more Zen asks his teacher a critical question.

"What does one do before enlightenment?" the student asked.

"Chop wood. Carry water," his master told him.

"What then," the student asked, "does one do after enlightenment?"

"Chop wood. Carry water," the Zen master replied.

My interpretation of this exchange, which will help anyone understand my Summit Mindset, is that we must be present in the moment of our tasks, but our mind can remain still and have the awareness and perception that keeps us from being preoccupied with work. If our job, however, gives us meaning and happiness, it is easier to gain balance in our lives and generate positive emotions. We avoid mental obstructions and worldly thinking to begin to understand what it is to simply *be* by using the Zen approach demonstrated in the previous koan. This may introduce us to the struggle between being and doing, but that does not mean we should stop our doing or discard its value. I think our problem in the modern world is that we get wrapped up in doing and accumulating things, and we lose the joy of just being. We can get trapped by the idea that if we just keep doing and doing, we will eventually arrive at a point where we will believe we have achieved a form of self-worth that will make us feel complete.

The Summit Mindset's assumption is that happiness occurs inside us or within an organization. You strive to do your best and be your best and make a conscious effort toward your happiness individually and as a part of your job or the organization. You also need to assume, as anyone does who reaches the summit and intends to stay there, that things will go bad. If you are aware of what brings you happiness, you are likely to have confidence that you will make it through the hard times and get back to enjoying your life. I confess to being shocked through the years by the number of people I have met who, in the latter half of their lives, are distraught and say they long ago stopped thinking about happiness. I find this incredibly common and sad. Such people have given up on chasing happiness and claim to lack the energy or determination to do what is necessary to achieve it. For me, rewarding work made me better and delivered greater belief in myself whenever I went through challenging times or confronted personal problems. I focused on my purpose and created more belief in myself, and out of that effort the Summit Mindset emerged. I have a formula for what I believe is happiness, and I will never, ever desert happiness.

What I had to acknowledge as I developed the Summit Mindset, however, was all the data that indicated the constant pursuit of happiness could backfire and lead to unhappiness. That's really what prompted me to find a formulation that included purpose and work. When we know our North Star, keep in mind that purpose is what drives us forward, and when we engage in the type of work that is meaningful, the possibility of happiness is far greater. If you are constantly pursuing only happiness and you fail, even if only occasionally, you are likely to experience sadness, disappointment, or self-blame. Being obsessed with happiness is likely to chase away the possibility you will ever find it. A study published in the journal *Emotion*, in fact, suggested our best chances for happiness involved the basic act of prioritizing positivity in our lives.[13]

---

13 Lahnna I. Catalino, Sara B. Algoe, and Barbara L. Fredrickson, "Prioritizing Positivity: An Effective Approach to Pursuing Happiness?" *Emotion* 14, no. 6 (December 2014): 1155–1161, https://www.ncbi.nlm.nih.gov/pmc/articles/PMC5533095/.

The researchers spent a decade looking for benefits of positive emotions in relation to mental and physical well-being. Their findings indicated that individuals who seek positivity by organizing their daily lives to include activities that make them feel good may experience more happiness than people who simply wait for it or work toward it without understanding how to achieve it. A key insight is that people can prioritize positivity in their schedules, and they can expect good outcomes from the practice, including a lowered risk of depression and more frequent occurrences of happiness and positive emotions. This offers a form of happiness that is readily accessible to us just by our basic daily decisions to include in our schedule those things that offer us some happiness or any positive feelings. The study concludes that seeking happiness might be a "delicate art" but that it may be a worthwhile pursuit. But it's not difficult to tell ourselves that if we like to run and running makes us happy, we will get up in the morning and go for a run. For me, these types of simple choices, combined with my fulfillment from meaningful work, have given me abundant happiness.

Because happiness may be the most discussed topic ever among humans, there is an abundance of theories and recommendations on how to capture the elusive emotion. The Summit Mindset places a premium on relationships. My belief has always been that there is nothing more important to our happiness than healthy relationships with family, friends, and our wider community. Focusing on our relationships and using them for comfort, friendship, and love will provide basic elements to achieving happiness. In fact, Harvard University recently published findings on an eighty-year study that examined the importance of relationships regarding mental health. Findings include data from 264 people traced by *Harvard Study of Adult Development* that showed happiness in relationships had a powerful influence on health, mental and physical.

Sociologists who have spent decades deconstructing happiness claim there are certain ways to ensure it happens to you. If your relationships are strong, you are more likely to have a support system to give you a soft place to fall and hide from stress. Social support, we are told, is an essential part of well-being. They also emphasize, as does the Summit Mindset, that we find a sense of purpose. My formulation, as I've said, is that for most of us that sense of purpose comes from work, which compels us to find something meaningful to do for a living or find a job we enjoy. Generally, though, a sense of purpose is about life goals and meaning. What direction will our lives take? If you don't have a purpose, you should spend time exploring your interests and passions while also looking for new subjects to learn more about. Consider also doing work to resolve injustices, the kind of project that might lead to the spreading of altruism across your town. Be open to experiences and ideas that you've never had, and see if they will take you anywhere pleasant, emotionally or physically.

Exercise, too, is an important part of the recipe for happiness in almost every analysis. Research shows that "even a little bit of exercise produces a happiness boost."[14] The data clearly indicate that only ten minutes a day of exercise led to much higher levels of happiness compared to people who never exercised. The most frequent and obvious result of regular exercise is an improved mood. The research also says that your mood will stay up and positive if you find a way to show gratitude. We can all find numerous things to be happy about in our daily lives, and the more we concentrate on those, the more happiness and life satisfaction we are likely to experience. Writing daily in a gratitude journal is a simple and inexpensive way to boost happiness. Gratitude for just being alive can lead to a cascade of appreciations for small things, too, and the joys of daily life will deliver happiness.

Happiness is also a primary contributor to personal optimism, which has been connected to an increased life span. A 2022 study by the Harvard T.H. Chan School of Public Health reported that higher levels of optimism were associated with longer lives, including

---

14   Darren E. R. Warburton, Crystal Whitney Nicol, and Shannon S. D. Bredin, "Health Benefits of Physical Activity: The Evidence," *Canadian Medical Association Journal* 174, no. 6 (March 14, 2006): 801–809, https://pubmed.ncbi.nlm.nih.gov/16534088/.

living beyond age ninety in women across racial and ethnic groups. The lead author of the study, Hayami Koga, a PhD student, said that the research suggests that the benefits of optimism may hold across diverse groups.

"A lot of previous work has focused on deficits or risk factors that increase the risks for diseases and premature death," Koga said. "Our findings suggest that there's value to focusing on positive psychological factors, like optimism, as possible new ways of promoting longevity and healthy aging across diverse groups."[15]

According to the findings, the 25 percent of the group who were the most optimistic were also likely to have a life span that was 5.4 percent longer. They also had a 10 percent greater likelihood of living beyond ninety years when compared to the 25 percent of the cohort who were the least optimistic. This was not a small or insubstantial body of data. Survey responses and information were analyzed from 159,255 participants in the Women's Health Initiative, which included postmenopausal women in the US. Enrollees ranged in age from fifty to seventy-nine and became a part of the study between 1993 and 1998. They were followed for as long as twenty-six years to achieve the findings data.

"We tend to focus on the negative risk factors that affect our health," Koga said. "It is also important to think about the positive resources, such as optimism, that may be beneficial to our health, especially if we see that these benefits are seen across racial and ethnic groups."

That happiness can be the genesis of optimism and extend our lives is probably not a shock. If they had been asked about the topic, I suspect the Abilene Boys could have offered a readily understandable explanation on how those two emotions worked to expand their enjoyment and long lives and led them back to the river after fifty-four years. Winfield James and Jim Pickard would have been forgiven if they

---

15   Todd Datz, "High Optimism Linked with Longer Life and Living Past 90 in Women across Racial, Ethnic Groups," Harvard T. H. Chan School of Public Health, June 8, 2022, https://www.hsph. harvard.edu/news/press-releases/optimism-longevity-women/.

had come up from the Texas Colorado and headed home after their dear friend Harry Caldwell had fallen gravely ill. Instead, they pressed on, knowing their canoe trip would deliver them happiness and that Harry would want them to continue. They pushed through thunderstorms and one-hundred-degree heat, mosquitos, snakes, river rapids, the canoe capsizing, and the muscle soreness and stiffness of men who had lived more than seven decades and were acting like boys. They did not, however, quit.

Winfield and Jim paddled against an onshore wind as they approached the Gulf of Mexico that warm day in 1991. Overhead, three Houston TV station news helicopters hovered, and a few dozen reporters and camera crews filmed as their canoe, which they had named *Prudence*, was paddled up onto the sand. Jim, sitting in the stern, put his paddle across his knees and raised both fists into the air with a smile even broader than the one he was wearing the morning they departed. Winfield stepped out of the boat and waded into the midst of admiring local officials and journalists amazed by the accomplishment. The Abilene Boys, by any measure, were happy, probably downright joyous. Their story spread widely and became the subject of an internationally acclaimed documentary film narrated by Walter Cronkite, which almost certainly inspired others to seek out happiness and the things that would bring them similar kinds of joy.

Happiness, I remain convinced, is almost always achievable. You can use the advice offered from experts and your own self-discipline to increase your personal well-being almost daily. Seek the positive, be confident in working through the negative, and know that happiness will return because you are mindful and conscious of what makes you happy. Don't think of getting there as a struggle but as a practice. Do the reps. Repeat the things that make you happy as often as you can and find your life's purpose. These techniques have worked for me and countless others and there is no reason they will not have the same results for you.

And remember, as the Abilene Boys showed us, happiness is a journey, not a destination.

Exercise:

- **Find Your Magic:** Have you answered the difficult question of what will truly make you happy? Envision your ideal life and what that might look like. Is it possible? Lay out the steps you might take to get there. Write your happiness scenario onto a card or whiteboard and put it in a location where you will see it every day. Does it still inspire you after several days, weeks, or months? Is it really what you want? If it is, figure out your first step and take it without hesitation. Believe that you can have what you dream. While you are working toward the big vision, what are the small things in your daily life that make you feel good and emotionally positive? Assess your personal well-being. Are you in a good place? List the little things that give you those good feelings and make certain to experience them often. Is it running or swimming or a good book or a new dress or a clean car or a piece of art? Be associated regularly with those things that make you feel good and lead to happiness.

CHAPTER TEN

COURAGE

Courage is not the absence of fear, but the triumph over it. The brave man is not he who does not feel afraid, but he who conquers that fear.

—NELSON MANDELA

A solitary man stood in front of a tank. A row of the armored vehicles came to a stop when the leading one was unable to continue. The driver maneuvered to the left, and the unidentified man stepped in the same direction to prevent any advance. He did not hesitate when the tank turned back to the right and stood between the gigantic rolling weapons system and Tiananmen Square. The forces of the People's Liberation Army were arriving at a public protest in China. Up to a million people, mostly students, had gathered in Central Beijing to protest the failure of China's single-party rule and its refusal to accept reforms that might lead to greater economic and political participation for the masses.

The unarmed man, wearing a white shirt, captured the entire world's attention on June 5, 1989. His determination was unwavering, though the world thought his judgment was foolish because he was certain to be killed or imprisoned by the government. Thousands were believed to have later been killed by the Chinese army, but the unknown man, defiant in front of military tanks, was pulled into the crowd by students, and disappeared. The tanks eventually rolled down Chang'an Avenue and put an end to the protests.

What he did, however, resonated around the world. The video of his singular defiance of an oppressive government was broadcast on virtually every media outlet in free countries. Photographer Stuart Franklin won a World Press Award for his photo "Tank Man," and *Time* magazine listed the unknown rebel as one of the "100 Most Important People of the 20th Century." *Life* magazine added the picture to its list of "100 Photos that Changed the World." There are unconfirmed reports Tank Man was later executed by the Chinese government, and other sources claim he is living anonymously in either Taiwan or Mainland China. His fate has never been confirmed.

Tank Man exhibited the kind of unrestrained courage that inspired millions. Guided by his principles and beliefs in the rights of individuals over government control, he acted in a manner that sent a message around the world about human dignity and the defiance of political oppression. There might be no way to know what influence Tank Man generated with his actions, but there are almost certainly leaders and protestors in other nations and in different conditions who were inspired by the fearless, unknown figure. My guess is that his decision has changed the world in ways that we will never completely comprehend but are still likely rippling on through the course of history.

I have often wondered about Tank Man through the years. Where did he get such courage? Everything he had accomplished—and his very life—was placed in jeopardy by his decision. Imagine if he had just finished years of medical school and was on the verge of beginning practice or a residency to launch a long career of helping the ill and infirm. Maybe he was married and had children and his family's future was put at risk by his actions, or he was the only child of a couple that had invested its entire savings in his education and aspirations for a career that might support his elders. Why did he do it? I suspect it was because whatever he had accomplished meant nothing to him if he had to live in a culture where he was not completely free. What might happen to him, he had decided, was less important than the greater cause.

Courage comes in many forms, and it is essential in almost everyone's life. We certainly cannot all be historic figures in Tiananmen Square, but we tend to be called upon to push through our adversities or to do things for others that might require us to exhibit strength and judgment we did not know we possessed. In the Summit Mindset, this means being ready every day to exhibit the bravery we need to succeed in life or to do whatever is necessary and within our power to make things better, even if that is only in our personal environments and daily endeavors. The summit is always more beautiful because of the struggle we experience during the climb and, I think, helps keep us motivated to continue our efforts to remain at the peak.

I am not sure we know exactly how to define courage. We know it is a personal characteristic that enables achievements of various kinds, and even inspires others, but we can't really measure it and determine if it comes in degrees or varying amounts. I think it is certainly about determination and the will to persevere when it would be much easier to sit down and try an alternative goal or surrender to obstacles you have decided simply cannot be overcome. We almost all find ourselves going through dark passages. I think we find our greater lessons come from our struggles and not from the glories of the winner's circle. Great individual courage like the Tank Man's is quiet and does not seek attention, but it comes from a will to persist and brings us to a better place, which might even be inspirational to people we don't even know but who have witnessed our struggles.

I have frequently relied on symbolic reminders of the importance of courage and how I had to find the will to live the Summit Mindset. While many of my peers think they are out of place in the boardroom, I have tattoos on my arms that are important to me, remind me of my personal story, and provide needed inspiration. At a certain point during a personal struggle, I was having trouble even getting out of bed, but while shaving one morning, I looked at my upper arm and decided I wanted a new bit of ink on my bicep. I had the word *Onward* tattooed there, and every morning when I look in the mirror to shave, I get a nudge from that ink to keep moving forward. When we are almost out of energy in our lives, courage is what helps us go onward. The word has become a kind of mantra for me and continues to guide my work and personal philosophy, including the formula for the Summit Mindset.

Public courage can require great character. Taking a principled stand can often mean you are alienating people on both sides of your beliefs. History is filled with people who have taken such a stand—Rosa Parks, Martin Luther King, Mahatma Gandhi, and, yes, the Tank Man of Tiananmen Square. Their words and actions can arguably be said to have set the course for profound political and cultural changes, but there are lesser-known individuals whose personal lives were altered by their convictions to closely held principles, though they had no great impact. The story of Lt. Ehren Watada, though not widely known, is an example of courage that caused him much personal sacrifice and criticism. People questioned his patriotism and character, and the course of his life was transformed, but he did not waver.

Commissioned as a first lieutenant in the US Army, Watada had served a year in South Korea before being redeployed to Fort Lewis, Washington, in 2006. Orders later arrived that he was to be sent to occupied Iraq. Watada, who had enlisted because he wanted to be a part of protecting the country after the attacks of 9/11, had grown uncertain over the explanations for the causes of the US invasion of Iraq. He began to read voraciously on the lack of evidence for weapons of mass destruction and spoke with numerous returning vets who described to him what they considered war crimes. When it came time for his unit to be rotated out for Operation Iraqi Freedom, Watada refused to board the plane and cited the international protocol of *command responsibility*, which can make an officer culpable for war crimes committed by troops operating under his orders. Watada volunteered to serve in Afghanistan because he viewed that as a mission with a purpose and that there were enemies of the US present and working against American interests. His commanders offered him a desk job in Iraq, but he said he was not resisting combat and simply did not believe our occupation of Iraq was morally justifiable.

Watada was putting much at risk with his decision. The army refused to give him the option of serving in Afghanistan, and his unwillingness to comply with orders meant a court martial and possible dishonorable discharge, which could mean difficulty with any career he might choose after his military service. Within the military ranks, he confronted tensions and criticisms, and parts of the Japanese American community, especially veterans, said he shamed those who had honorably served. Watada attempted to resign from the army and wrote a letter to his commanding officers saying that he was "wholeheartedly opposed to the continuing war in Iraq," and he mentioned the deceptions involved in justifying the invasion. His letter cited the Downing Street Memo from the British government, which claimed the "war in Iraq was inevitable" and that the "intelligence and facts were being fixed around the policy" of war.

The army refused to accept the young lieutenant's resignation and charged him with conduct unbecoming an officer and a gentleman and a separate count for "missing movement," which was related to his refusal to board the bus with his troops to the airport. If convicted in a general court martial, Watada would have faced up to seven years in prison, or a dismissal from the army, which is the equivalent of a dishonorable discharge. His attorney claimed that the "conduct unbecoming" allegations were an attempt to silence him and other public critics of the war and were related to interviews he had granted to explain his resistance. Lt. Watada, though, said he would have refused to go to Iraq regardless of the charges he faced.

"When you are looking your children in the eye in the future," he told a reporter, "or when you are at the end of your life, you want to look back on your life and know that at a very important moment, when I had the opportunity to make the right decisions, I did so, even knowing there were negative consequences."[16]

---

16   Jeremy Brecher and Brendan Smith, "Lieutenant Watada's War against the War," Jeremy Brecher.org, June 26, 2006, https://www.jeremybrecher.org/lieutenant-watada%E2%80%99s-war-against-the-war/.

The court martial ended in a mistrial over a legal maneuver regarding Watada's admission of guilt. When the army rescheduled its prosecution, the lieutenant's lawyers insisted he was being exposed to double jeopardy. An appeals court held in his favor, and the entire case was later dropped. He was given an "other than honorable discharge," which is considered the least favorable separation available for officers leaving the army under involuntary conditions. Regardless of how anyone might feel about Watada's politics, his choice to resist deployment was an undeniable act of courage. He put his career, freedom, and reputation on the line because they were less important to him than a principle of right and wrong regarding the US invasion of Iraq.

Most of us are never confronted with such a difficult situation as Lt. Watada. We can, however, find ways to live courageously in our daily lives. The Summit Mindset teaches us to conduct ourselves in a manner that expresses strength and determination to reach our goals and be servant leaders. This doesn't mean we are waiting for some dramatic moment in which to act with bravery and save the day. Instead, I have always suggested simple acts like being accountable and responsible while growing and learning. We need to help others when we are able and practice gratitude for all we have been given. When it's possible, we must learn how to forgive, say we are sorry when appropriate, and make goals for ourselves while also keeping our commitment to those who are relying on our actions. Courage isn't just about a solitary moment; it's also a process and a way to live, which makes it an integral part of the Summit Mindset.

True courage is a combination of many factors. We need to be brave before we can have confidence in whatever we are trying to accomplish. Imagine having a dream for a business or a piece of art you want to create but you are afraid to start. Fear of failure can stifle the greatest ambitions and never give them a chance to live. Confidence comes from experience, performing in a fulfilling manner, and finishing a task you have set for yourself, but you cannot acquire confidence without first exercising courage. The first step is to take whatever chance is before you, with the courage necessary to start out. In that journey, you will experience many successes and failures and you will learn from these. That education will give you confidence to deal with anything that you might confront in the future. Until you have the courage to take a risk and try something new and different, you will never acquire the confidence that comes from experience. Most great achievements in our lives begin with our singular acts of courage.

As I developed the Summit Mindset during my business life, I always considered courage to be a prerequisite to confidence. You simply cannot get to confidence without the courage to try something the first time. Having courage allows you, no matter how you might think or feel about yourself and the opportunities before you, regardless of the various outcomes, to be willing to take whatever risks and step toward what you want. You put comfort and security at risk to get what you want. Confidence comes later through performance and effort and does not mysteriously become a part of your character without the intentional effort to be brave. Most of us struggle to deal with our fears, and many fears accumulate in daily life at home and work. Our greatest fear tends to be the disappointment that comes from failure. By asserting the courage required to take the risk—using what the Summit Mindset refers to as smart actions—we give ourselves chances to fulfill dreams and make any risk worth it. Failure and mistakes are how we grow, and without them, we learn nothing. Trying is of far greater importance than failing. Make the effort. Stumble and fall. Treat your wounds, physical or psychological, and then try again. The process to succeed begins with courage, and through experience comes confidence.

Through years of trying and failing and succeeding, I came to understand there were certain dynamics that repeated as I put forth the necessary effort to achieve my dreams. The following is not a complete list, but I do see these factors and behaviors as essential to exercising courage. Confidence and courage and bravery are all a part of the whole cloth of success. These bits of advice, I am confident, can help anyone. They became foundational planks for me as I formulated the Summit Mindset.

THE CALCULUS OF COURAGE

1. **Don't Quit:** There are always going to be obstacles and road-blocks. If you turn back when they are first encountered, you will go nowhere. Regardless of whatever the setback might be, press on. You might be moving toward your goal more slowly than you had hoped, but chances are good you will still be making progress, and even a little progress becomes movement of consequence.

2. **Embrace Failure:** Put your arms around failure and learn what it teaches you. Understand your mistakes so they won't be repeated. Think of failure as an education. Courage is knowing that it is likely to happen, but it won't keep you from your pursuit.

3. **Manage Fear:** There is always something to be afraid of, but don't let it inhibit you or make you timid. Doubts are normal and often legitimate, but don't concentrate on them. Acknowledge them but resist letting them influence your decisions. Overcome your own skepticisms. Believe in your dream and your ability to get there.

4. **Be Clear About Your Goals:** Nothing is more important in exercising courage than knowing what you want to achieve. Detail the steps you will take to get going in the right direction. What does success look like? Are there efforts you can make in preparation that will reduce the risk and raise your courage? Is your goal realistic for your current level of preparation or is more work needed to get ready?

5. **Do Not Settle:** Always climb in the direction of the summit. Know you can get there. Do not settle for some lesser version of your dream. The courageous know what they must do to build the life they have dreamed. Believe in yourself and be confident that you deserve exactly what you want and that there is no rea-son to compromise your standards or your vision of the future.

6. **Be You:** That might seem simplistic, but there is no reason for you to seek validation. You know who you are and what you are capable of. Don't perform for others. Courage means being authentic with everyone in your path. Be transparent and real, and people will sense your courage and may even want to help. Understand your own self-worth.

7. **Inventory Your Assets:** Know your strengths. Understand how they can be leveraged. What are your skill sets? Identify the characteristics you've exhibited in the past when you were successful. How will you use these factors to build up your courage? Be optimistic because that feeds our courage. Envision a person with your talents getting what they want. The more you know about yourself, the fewer chances you will be required to take.

8. **Don't Avoid Challenges:** These are there for a reason. You must be tested and overcome obstacles. There is no growth without challenge. Having courage means acknowledging that what you fear may simply be a random idea that has entered your consciousness without any basis in fact. Do not let fear drive your decisions. Give it no control or influence. Don't waste time worrying. Act and move confidently toward your goals.

9. **Reduce Stress:** Nothing affects performance as insidiously as stress does. Try to manage internal fretting. Accept that there are certain things you can deal with and that others are beyond your control and should not cause you anxiety. Eat right, exercise, sleep well. Consider meditation. Take as much care of your mind as you do your body. Stress distracts and destroys you and your ideas and dreams.

10. **Ask for Help:** This may be the hardest thing for any entrepreneur or dreamer. But it's important to accept that you don't know as much as you need to know and there are others who can help with information and advice. Don't be afraid to ask someone with more experience. If you are starting up a business, you

will almost certainly need to be asking for investors. Ask also for knowledge from people who know more than you and might be able to help with connections and expertise.

We all need courage every day of our lives. Even easy tasks can become overwhelming in certain circumstances. Think of the single mother with two children to raise who confronts bills for rent and school clothes, food and medicine, but has never had a chance for her own education. What happens if she gives up? Her children might become victims of her failure and end up in lives of reduced opportunities. She doesn't quit. The mother wakes, prepares breakfast, gets her children off to school, and heads to work, trying to excel and earn a raise or find the money and energy to take night classes to advance her education and improve her career options. How many parents struggle daily with these challenges but never give up because they have the courage needed to make it through difficult circumstances?

Courage is not always dramatic. It is a basic act of character that makes most of life's accomplishments possible by the sheer exertion of will. There are, though, individuals whose singular choices set standards that help to define what it is to be human and to inspire those of us who are dealing with lesser matters in our lives. We sometimes see these people in the news or we read about their bravery in stories. Our minds race to comprehend the choices these people made, what their logic was when they took these great risks. Did they act before they thought through their decision? There are those among us who appear unafraid, or maybe they are simply willing to live with whatever the outcome is when they take a great chance to help others or turn around a terrible situation. They are, perhaps, guided by their hearts and circumstance and not logic. Courage, though, whatever its motivation, is the requirement of their actions.

One of the bravest acts I've ever heard about occurred after the earthquake and tsunami that destroyed the nuclear power plant in Fukushima, Japan. Three reactors melted down and began to spew radiation into the air and water. The damage incurred was such that there was no way for machinery and mechanical engineering to clean up the irradiated water and construction materials. Workers needed to put on special suits to protect them from radioactivity inside the facilities, but there was no guarantee of complete protection. The Japanese government set standards for exposure, but there was a significant possibility of radiation causing cancers later in life for the employees of the Tokyo Electric Power Company (TEPCO). Explosions and fires also increased the level of danger for workers going inside to remove water and debris and attempting to seal off reactors with melted cores.

As he watched the crisis unfolding on the news every day, seventy-two-year-old Yasuteru Yamada was struck by the bravery of the young workers walking into the reactor buildings to carry out their daily assigned responsibilities. Yamada had spent twenty-eight years working as an engineer in the metals industry and understood many of the complexities involved in the dangerous remediation of the Fukushima nuclear complex. The goal was to bring the three crippled reactors into a stable shutdown, but the timeline to complete the work was unknown, and as the days and weeks and months rolled onward, there was increasing concern about health issues for young workers entering the plant.

Yamada believed what he was witnessing would confound the Fukushima tragedy. Youth ought not be sacrificed, and he had an idea. He would assemble a group of volunteer engineers, professionals, construction workers, and others over the age of sixty to conduct cleanup operations inside of reactor buildings. His generation, he believed, needed to stand up and do its part to stabilize the situation at the nuclear generator. Yamada called his brave group the Skilled Veterans Corps, which he built up using emails, phone calls, and social media messages on Twitter. There was no shortage of positive responses, despite the dangers to be faced.

"I am seventy-two, and on average I have thirteen to fifteen years yet to live," Yamada told a reporter. "Even if I were exposed to radiation, cancer could take twenty or thirty years longer to develop. Therefore, us older ones have less chance of getting cancer. I will be dead before cancer gets me."[17]

The Japanese government and the power company executives at TEPCO were, initially, resistant to his idea. One federal official referred to the Skilled Veterans Corps as the "Kamikaze Corps," a reference to the World War II pilots from Japan who flew their planes into American ships in an act of suicide. But quickly, Yamada had lined up 270 volunteers to take on the risky and brutal jobs, working for free. TEPCO and the government relented and began to see the effort as a kind of Red Cross of civil engineering experts who were all willing to put their lives on the line. As the word spread, the enlistees grew in number, and there were soon more than two thousand willing to share the risks across the dangerous task list and various projects required for remediation.

The altruism of Yamada and his contemporaries never got truly deployed at the Fukushima plant. The corps of volunteers stood at the ready, but TEPCO and the government decided the first wave of remediation was to be managed by the younger workers at the facility. Fifty of them stayed behind after management had evacuated 750 other technicians. The fifty even lived within the stricken complex in an earthquake-proofed building at the center of the complex and worked on rotating shifts to carry out procedures to reduce the contamination of the surrounding environment, prevent fires, and manage any potential meltdown of the reactors. In about a week after the tsunami, there were more than one thousand firefighters, soldiers, technical experts, and others who were actively engaged in attempting to mitigate the plant's problems.

Yasuteru Yamada's Skilled Veterans Corps for Fukushima was never called to duty. Membership did, however, remain active in efforts to monitor the plant and act as liaisons for concerned citizens and residences around the plant, and they attended government meetings to offer input to develop plans and policies around decommissioning

17 Roland Buerk, "Japan Pensioners Volunteer to Tackle Nuclear Crisis," BBC News, May 31, 2011, https://www.bbc.com/news/world-asia-pacific-13598607.

Fukushima. They also were present and involved in public meetings, offered expert testimony and advice, and remained willing to give the ultimate sacrifice if it were necessary to protect their country and community. Yamada lived just three more years after the tragedy, but his example of hope and sacrifice inspired the courage of many people still conducting remediation at the Fukushima nuclear complex, and in his fellow countrymen who saw themselves in his commitment to service and the protection of the younger generation.

Yasuteru Yamada's version of courage was heroic, but most of us are not called to that level of commitment. Instead, we try to exercise everyday courage to do the difficult things necessary for ourselves and our families. The courage that masses of people find to exercise in their daily lives is much more important than individual heroism because it can have a broader impact. This might also be called grit or determination. I examined numerous ideas surrounding the concept of courage as I was thinking about the Summit Mindset. The essential definition is a variation on the belief that people respond fearlessly in the face of anxiety and the worry that they are confronting. I am not sure that is the best description because the wise and aware person cannot dispose of their fears. Those individuals are aware of what they are, try to manage their effect on decisions, and move forward to do what they believe is necessary. To be courageous, you must understand what you are afraid of but refuse to allow that knowledge to paralyze you.

A significant amount of research has been conducted by educators and analysts of various disciplines to define and categorize types of courage. There might be as many definitions as there are experts, but in my reading and experience, I think four different types of everyday courage encompass the human experience.

KINDS OF COURAGE

1. **Intellectual Courage:** We are daily confronted with common knowledge and accepted understandings of various social dynamics, traditions, and even cultural standards. Things

change, though, and new ideas are generated that challenge our outdated ways of thinking. Our obligation is to learn and understand when norms are challenged and, when appropriate, have the intellectual courage to embrace the new approaches, including systems of belief. There will always be new research and practices that conflict with current methods and, when they are improvements, we need to accept what they provide. Not much is harder than recognizing the limitations of our own thinking, which prevents us from being open to new findings and recommendations. Cultures and professions are always evolving, and some alterations are revolutionary. Have the intellectual courage to not be afraid and to be a person who leads when the time is right. Challenge old assumptions when your experience and research convince you that they are wrong.

2. **Moral Courage:** Think of people throughout history who have chosen to do the right thing even when the odds against them were overwhelming. Moral courage is about standing up for what is right and challenging what you know to be morally wrong. The actions of a person exercising moral courage tend to be focused on the greater good. Rosa Parks and Martin Luther King Jr. exhibited the moral courage to lead their country into a transformative change that produced equal rights and inclusion for people of all races. Harvey Milk, who was elected San Francisco city supervisor, was the first openly gay politician elected to public office in California. He fought anti-gay initiatives and got a measure passed that banned discrimination in public accommodations, housing, and employment based upon sexual orientation. Milk was assassinated for his beliefs, but his moral courage led to sweeping cultural and political changes in America. He was posthumously awarded the Presidential Medal of Freedom in 2009. Moral courage is knowing what's right, doing what's right, and risking the consequences. It is likely the most difficult form of courage to exercise. The Summit Mindset

encourages each of us to cultivate our moral courage because we will be strengthened by righteousness in all our endeavors.

3. **Courage of Empathy:** We need to find the will to be open to and feel empathy for other people. This may not sound like a form of courage, but it is much easier for us to default to our personal biases and use our assumptions to hide out from notions or personalities that make us uncomfortable and challenge our thinking or behavior. Letting go of your control will allow you to empathize and maybe even learn something new. Try to see the world through another person's eyes. Have the courage to try to understand their feelings and to open yourself up to a relationship that might be of mutual benefit. This is a basic way to improve communication, which can lead to enhanced motivation in the workplace. Leaders must have the courage to express empathic concern, too. When people trust you and your decisions, they are more likely to collaborate to accomplish more and take risks. I don't believe any of us can reach our summits without a significant degree of empathy and you cannot acquire empathy without some courage.

4. **Courage of Discipline:** Discipline as a form of courage is required for almost all achievement. You need to stay focused on goals and targets that are part of your vision. Maintaining clarity in the face of opposition, whether that is organized or simply circumstance, is essential to overcoming odds. Discipline gives you the determination to take the next step in your climb up the summit. Develop endurance and flexibility because they are both dynamics that lay the foundation for discipline and the courage you need for execution of plans. Try to do something courageous every day that moves you closer to your vision. Discipline yourself to constantly work toward your goal, even if each action you take is small; the cumulative result will be the realization of your dream. Don't let emotions control you, and always be willing to consider compromise if it facilitates what you want

to achieve, especially if it also is assisting someone else's efforts that have value.

I believe in one other form of courage, too, though it is generally not talked about in academic circles. By concentrating on the more important intellectual and emotional forms of courage, we tend to overlook the physical form. People are generally able to avoid the need for physical courage because we can evade situations that require us to put our physical selves in jeopardy, though that is not always possible. We are not soldiers, though, or construction workers or scientists involved in dangerous projects, nor do we want to end up in dangerous situations with criminals or other bad actors who might force us to defend ourselves or put us into life-threatening circumstances. Physical courage, though, can be required of us when we least expect it. More benign forms might be someone working through therapy to recover from an injury or having the determination to acquire fitness and lose weight after decades of bad habits. Physical courage may very well be the foundational form of courage you need to make your effort to take on the Summit Mindset and become the person you want to be.

Countless books and academic and religious studies try to define and understand courage. No single description applies across all eventualities involving people. I think, generally, we know it when we see it, and often we don't recognize it in the daily mundane habits that comprise individual courage and long-term achievements. There are obvious examples of bravery that stand out, of doing the right thing at great physical or reputational risk in hopes of results that cannot be calculated. Most of us learn the difference between right and wrong from our cultures, even in the absence of parents. What do we do, then, when confronted with complex decisions? How does one person find the courage to do what is required and another shirks their moral obligations?

Stanley Lord found himself in that position just after midnight on April 15, 1912. You have probably never heard of him because history has almost disposed of his story. He would be totally unknown if not for the fact that his actions have served as a countermeasure to the courage that led others to act. Lord was the captain of a ship in the Northern Atlantic that dark, cold April night. The *Californian* was reportedly less than twenty kilometers away from the unsinkable *Titanic*, and Lord and his crew were able to see the massive cruise liner on the horizon through the clear, starlit night. A night watch sailor informed Captain Lord that the *Titanic* was firing off distress rockets, though Lord later said he had no idea they were signals calling for help.

Lord did not act. The North Atlantic was filled with icebergs, and there was great risk in maneuvering his ship through them in the darkness. The decision was to be one he'd regret his entire life. British inquiries of the tragedy later concluded that if Lord had pushed his ship through the ice floes that he might have saved many, if not all the passengers in the icy waters of the Atlantic. Instead, 1,726 died. Captain Lord did not even bother to awaken his wireless operator to contact the distressed *Titanic*, nor did he alter his ship's course to head in the direction of the stricken vessel. A researcher of the sinking concluded that Lord decided that the hazard to himself and his command was too great to justify responding, so the *Californian* did nothing.

Arthur Rostron, captain of the *Carpathia*, fixed the position of his ship at approximately one hundred kilometers distant from the sinking *Titanic*. His wireless operator had rushed into the captain's cabin and told him the great ship was in distress and was calling for help. Harold Cottam, who was messaging the *Titanic* about telegraphs for its passengers that were backing up, took in the new international distress signal for one of the first times in history. "SOS," which later became abbreviation for "save our souls" and "save our ship," filled Cottam with great fear. Obviously, he would have found the signal difficult to believe, but he was frighteningly certain of its accuracy and convinced Captain Rostron, whose first words were to issue a command to his first officer, Horace Dean.

"Mr. Dean," he said, "turn this ship around."

Rostron worked out a course for his ship and then cut off steam to every operation other than the engines, which accelerated the *Carpathia* up to sixteen knots, at least one knot above the speed for which it was designed. Extra lookouts were posted all around the ship to watch for icebergs as she made her dangerous passage toward the potential victims of the collision. The risks to Rostron and his vessel were significant, and he later told a historian that he felt that "some other hand than mine was on the helm that night."

The *Carpathia* and crew arrived at the correct coordinates about ninety minutes after the great vessel had slipped beneath the waves. Had they not noticed a green flare from a lifeboat, Rostron might have been inclined to sail away and believe there had been a mistake or miscommunication. Instead, his ship spent hours gathering up survivors while his crewmen worked through a sea littered with bodies of the frozen and drowned. Captain Rostron gathered up 705 survivors and quickly took a heading for New York. Lord and his *Californian* had finally come to understand what was happening and steamed to the scene when daylight arrived and after it was confirmed the *Titanic* had sunk. Captain Lord's crew spent their time gathering up bodies, a process that would require other recovery efforts and lasted almost three weeks.

History has not been kind to Captain Stanley Lord. He spent the remainder of his life trying to clear his name, and researchers and boards of inquiry have suggested that his ship might not have been as close as reported. A phenomenon of *cold water illusions* was cited to explain visuals, perhaps magnification of starlight on the water. There were also reports of ghost ships in the area and that, perhaps, one of those was likely what was believed to be the *Titanic*. Inaccurate records of ships' logs, though, make it impossible to know. Lord's most damning decision, which he could never escape, was that he failed to awaken his wireless operator even after his crew was bringing him information that needed further scrutiny. At least a few official reports indicated that even if Lord had immediately set a course for the *Titanic*, it would have been too late to save passengers.

The difference between Lord and Captain Arthur Rostron remains distinct through history, however. One showed immediate bravery and almost fearless judgment. The other was dangerously circumspect, and partially blamed for the loss of life. There is sufficient sadness in the tragedy that was once called "a night to remember," but we are always left to wonder if it had to result in such a dark, unimaginable outcome. We also have to accept that there are few stories that offer greater proof of the importance of courage in our lives. The lesson for everyone is to daily cultivate and express our courage in every small and possible manner.

There is always a chance in our lives that we might arrive in circumstances that require courage. It is both worthy and noble to prepare ourselves for that possibility in case we are ever needed.

Exercise:

- **Practice Courage:** Think of the day just concluded and consider where you might have shown more courage and character. Was there a moment when you could have made a difference for someone if you had spoken or intervened? Go through your past week or month and identify situations, large or small, where your courage could have positively changed things. Make a list of your personal strengths. What do you have to contribute that can be helpful when courage is required in a situation? Can you think of habits or gestures or comments you offer daily that build your character and help fortify your efforts to create and increase your personal courage?

CHAPTER ELEVEN

THE SUMMIT MINDSET FORMULATION

- **You Versus You:** Our perception of ourselves can limit our accomplishments and happiness. To succeed, we must win this conflict and overcome the limitations we place on ourselves, which are often based wrongly on our acceptance of how others see us. Work to defy expectations you have attached to your life. Know that you can do the work required to become what you dream of being.

- **Do the Reps:** We become our habits. Repeat the good ones— over and over, every day, if possible. Big improvements come out of small behaviors in business or our personal lives. Make these positive habits a part of your day. Weightlifters don't go to the gym when they are struck by the mood, and musicians don't wait for a moment of inspiration. They do the work. You can start today by developing good habits and disciplines and exercising them every day. Progress will appear.

- **Find Your North Star:** Determine what moves you and is greater than you. A company needs a purpose just as much as a person. Find the big vision for your life or your business. Work toward that dream while also taking the habitual steps in your daily life to find happiness in the mileposts you pass as you move in the direction of your big goal. Your North Star can guide your life and your business or career. Know who you are and what you want to be a part of, and plan to get there.

- **The Inside-Out Job:** Start your transition by performing the Inside-Out job. Examine yourself for strengths and weaknesses. Ask the hard question of yourself or your company: What do I suck at? If you suck at something important that is needed for your goals and to follow your North Star, take the necessary steps to get better at it. Self-examination should lead to self-improvement. Nobody is good at everything. No business is completely optimized for success. Keep looking inward, and the outward expressions of achievement will arrive faster.

- **Four Pillars:** Identify the four pillars upon which you will base your life, career, or business. These are the four most important elements to guide us to the summit and to happiness and achievement. Are they your faith? What about your family and friends? Maybe work is one of the cornerstones that hold up an important pillar for you. Public service and philanthropy are often a pillar for people. Work, faith, family, and others make for a fine set of pillars for almost anyone's life. Give some thought to these dynamics in your life and the ones that matter the most.

- **Smart Actions:** Don't just intend to do the things necessary to accomplish your tasks and move closer to your goals. Take smart actions as often as possible. Be certain you are doing something that will make a difference in your immediate project or your life. Don't do things to just be busy. Remember that intentions are not actions. Identify your intentions and then act on them with smart tactics and efforts that move them closer to reality. The greater the number of smart actions a person or a business takes, the sooner success arrives. It is not complicated.

- **Acknowledge Adversity:** Know that rain is going to fall. A storm will always come, but it will also always pass. Be prepared as you climb to the summit. Stand on your pillars. Even if one is weak and caused the adversity, the other three will hold you up until you can begin repair on the one that is leaning or cracked. Adversity is inevitable, but when you are prepared, it cannot stop you from reaching the summit or remaining above the storms. Remember to use adversity to grow stronger and steelier for the next time it materializes in your life.

- **Maintain Constructive Dissatisfaction:** The most successful and often the most fulfilled people are those who are constructively dissatisfied. They always want to be a little better, smarter, healthier, happier, or more productive. Learn to go back over what you have accomplished and review the tape. Find what you did well and where improvements could be made, and make recalibrations. Then make more recalibrations. Constantly recalibrate until you feel you or your company has done the best possible job, and then move to the next task using the same approach.

- **No Finish Line:** Live as if there is no finish line. Even after you have won, keep going. There is more to do, to see, to accomplish. Find the next project or future friend, or dream another big dream about a business or a charity. Always press onward to more interesting activities, endeavors, and improvements that are both personal and business. Maintain a lifelong curiosity that will lead you beyond any finish lines. Never, ever, ever quit.

TENETS OF THE SUMMIT MINDSET

The Summit is where I have built my house.

———

Most people climb to the Summit and descend. I will die at the Summit.

———

The adversity at times is overwhelming, but it keeps me hungry.

———

Most days it humbles me.

———

Many days you can be snowed in, waking up only to dig out and hold on until the storm passes.

———

Other days you're totally fogged in with zero visibility.

———

Finally, some days there is nothing but blue skies as far as the eye can see.

————

These days the Summit is filled with peace and a total sense of calm.

————

In these moments, you realize just how amazing the Summit is and that's why I built my house there.

————

Some days I'm hungry.

————

Like a caged lion who hasn't eaten for two weeks and is ready to pounce on its prey.

————

Day to day you can never predict the climate at the Summit.

————

My biggest learning is that I can never control the climate.

————

I will always lean into the climate that is continuously changing.

————

I encourage you to build your house at the Summit and live here with me.

————

For I am home here at the Summit.

————

For this is life!

> *Scott Miller, dad, husband, brother, uncle,*
> *friend, global citizen, and dream chaser.*

No Finish Line/Let's Go!

ABOUT THE AUTHORS

SCOTT MILLER has been a CEO and executive leader of several global beverage companies. He began his career on the warehouse floor at Pepsi and learned the industry from the front line to the boardroom. His reputation as an executive was built around a people first approach to conducting business and dealing with customers and vendors. Miller's reputation has been one of innovation and market expansion through Corporate Social Responsibility and a culture of community involvement for his companies. His most recent accomplishment was leading the growth and acquisition of Essentia, a national bottled water brand, to global food and beverage leader Nestlé. *The Summit Mindset* is his first book.

JAMES C. MOORE is a *New York Times* best-selling author of seven books, which include topics from presidential politics to medicine, technology, and science fiction. He is an Emmy-winning former TV news correspondent who has also worked for cable news networks as an on-air political analyst and opinion writer. His documentary films have won international festivals, and he was frequently named the best TV reporter in Texas by the Associated Press, UPI, Houston Press Club, and the Texas Headliners' Foundation.